HIGHER AND LOWER

An Illustrated History of the Higher and Lower Division of Llanrhidian

including the villages of Llanrhidian, Penclawdd, Three Crosses and their neighbouring communities

R N Cooper

Illustrations by the author

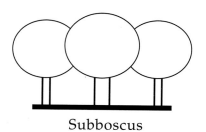

Subboscus

ISBN No. 0 9534523 0 1
Published by Subboscus, The Lodge, Park Road, Penclawdd, Swansea, SA4 3FH
© 1998 R N Cooper
All drawing by, and copyright of, the author.
Typeset in Palatino and printed by Sayce Brothers, Caxton House, High Street,
Llandrindod Wells, Powys LD1 6AG Tel 01597 822169

Contents

Acknowledgements

No work of this nature can be attempted without the support of a great many people. Throughout the parish of Llanrhidian, both Higher and Lower Divisions, a great number of people have proffered information, help and encouragement for which I am immensely grateful. Outside the parish, I must mention Mr Nigel Wassell, whose compendious knowledge of the local canal and railway has been invaluable, and Dr Jonathan Kissock for his insights into the medieval development of north Gower. The staff of many archive sources have been unfailingly helpful in research - I should mention the National Library of Wales Manuscripts Department, the West Glamorgan Archive Service at Swansea, the staff of the Swansea University library and the staff of Swansea Central Reference Library. The use of the Cambrian Index in Swansea Library has been especially helpful. Mr Rowan Guy, clerk to the Llanrhidian Higher Community Council, has kindly given me details relating to some more recent aspects of local history.

Anyone who has embarked on a local history will know that a certain level of tolerance is needed from those nearest and dearest to them. I have been fortunate in securing from my wife, Sue, not only tolerance but active encouragement and support in contemplating and preparing this work - if any credit accrues from this book she deserves some share of it.

HIGHER AND LOWER

When *'A Dark and Pagan Place'* was published, in 1986, it was the result of some ten years' research into the history of the district around Penclawdd, Llanmorlais and Crofty. Such studies are necessarily parochial in nature and, in selecting the information needed for the book, much was put to one side as of no interest to readers with a purely parochial interest. Research has carried on since 1986 and new evidence has come to light on the 'dark and pagan' place. But as this study has continued a great bulk of historical information has accumulated, not only about Penclawdd, but also a wider area. This area is Llanrhidian. Not just the little village nestling at the edge of the vast marshes of the Burry Estuary but the whole of its original parish stretching from Dunvant in the east to Weobley Castle in the west. Research made it increasingly clear that this huge parish has been, until relatively recent times, one entity. To understand the story of any one part of the parish without reference to the greater whole is not truly possible.

'Higher and Lower' is an attempt to draw together the diverse strands of the history of all Llanrhidian's parish, both higher and lower parts. Today the two halves of the parish seem to some like 'chalk and cheese', so different are they. At one time, however, they were part of a single economic organism, based on the manorial system of the late medieval period. The story of how they became so different reveals important truths about the way Wales has developed over the centuries particularly with regard to the influence of the English and of industrialism. 'Higher' and 'Lower' are not just convenient terms that make for a book title, they are a vital part of the story. 'Higher' and 'Lower' are expressions common in medieval history in Wales; they usually reflect the difference between the poor pasture of the hills and the richer farmlands lower down, the inferior lands assigned to the Welsh and the more favoured fields taken by the English. In Llanrhidian it also led to one part of the parish progressing with the centuries and the other part lapsing back into a rural idyll. The theme of 'higher and lower' is even seen within the communities. Both Penclawdd and Llanrhidian villages have, at times, been described as in higher and lower parts. It is likely that within the perceptions of people living at the top end or the bottom end of the village there were more subtle perceptions about the differences between the inhabitants.

The approach of this book is to present themes central to the understanding of the history of the area in a series of short, illustrated, essays. Once again, as in *'A Dark and Pagan Place'*, there has had to be selection of material and much has been discarded. This is a painful operation but the purpose has been to avoid cluttering the story with too many facts. It is to be hoped that, in spite of many ommissions, the sense of Llanrhidian as whole, with its complex history, will be perceived.

Wern Fabian Farm,
Llanmorlais c1890.
Photo courstesy
Mrs Mary Phillips

1

Llanrhidian Parish - How the Land Lies

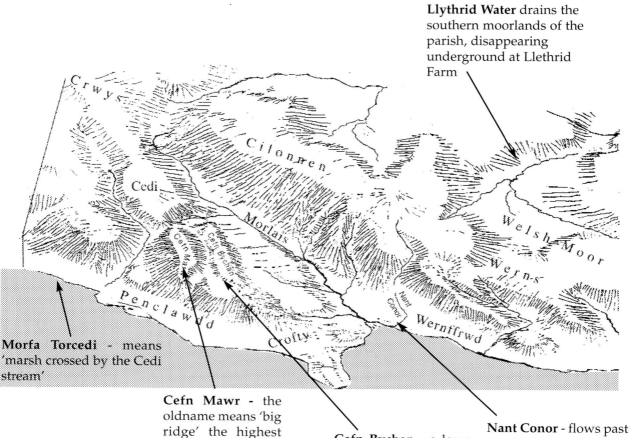

Llythrid Water drains the southern moorlands of the parish, disappearing underground at Llethrid Farm

Morfa Torcedi - means 'marsh crossed by the Cedi stream'

Cefn Mawr - the oldname means 'big ridge' the highest part of the hill above Penclawdd

Cefn Bychan - a lower ridge beside Cefn Mawr. The earliest settlement was between the two ridges.

Nant Conor - flows past Cwm Cynnar Farm. 'Cynnar' and 'Conor' are clearly of the same origin.

Wern - means 'a wet place with alder trees'. This is a frequent name on sloping land throughout the east end of the parish reflecting the wet and boggy nature of the ground. Note the names 'Wernhalog', 'Wern Cefnbychan' and 'The Wern' near Llanmorlais. South of Wernffrwd a whole hillside used to called 'Werns' and the stream or 'ffrwd' flowing off the Werns was call the 'Wernffrwd' - hence the name of the village where the stream joins the estuary.

The Burry Estuary has been a shallow tidal water with sands and marshes throughout its recorded history. As a source of food (fish and cockles) and extensive grazing it has been an area vital to the economy of the parish.

Cilifor Top - at 118 m one of the most imposing hills in the parish though by no means the highest.

The parish of Llanrhidian has a rich diversity of landscapes. Many features have lost the names originally given them but some of the names have survived. On this page many of these names are revived alongside some of those still in common use. These names often explain themselves when translated.

Broad Pool - where the clay on the moors is thick enough to stop the water seeping away underground.

Cefn Bryn - rising to 178 metres, the highest point in the parish. The north slope is a large area of moorland, common to the parishes of Llanrhidian, Nicholaston, Penmaen, Penrice and Reynoldston.

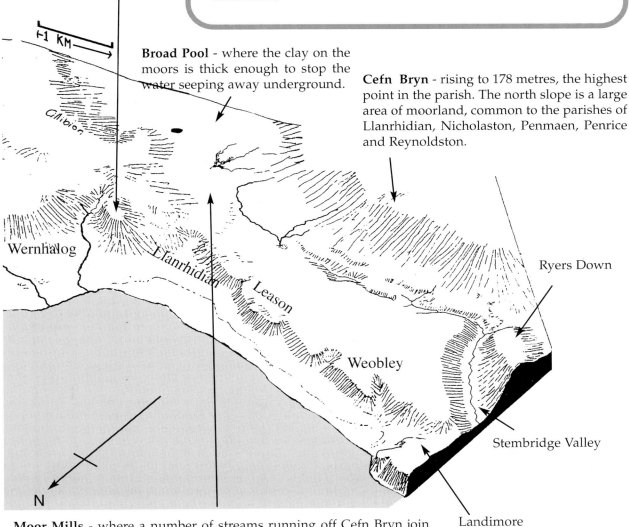

⊢1 KM⊣

Gilibron

Wernhalog

Llanrhidian

Leason

Weobley

Ryers Down

Stembridge Valley

N

Landimore

Moor Mills - where a number of streams running off Cefn Bryn join and disappear underground. They reappear by Llanrhidian Church. A number of other streams flowing off the moors disappear in the same way and reappear nearer the Burry estuary.

3

Llanrhidian - the Rocks Beneath

The rocks of Llanrhidian all outcrop along a line (known as 'the strike') trending WNW to ESE. As a result all the main ridges and streams tend to follow this direction for all or part of their course. The faults, or cracks, in these rocks are at right angles to the strike and occur mostly in the eastern half of the parish.

Millstone Grit - the rather soft and shaly beds of Millstone Grit in Gower rather belie their name and provided no millstones but some hard sandstones give rise to pronounced ridges protruding towards the Burry estuary. The little ridge of Llanelen and the impressive bulk of Cilifor Top are such ridges at the northern and southern edges respectively of the grits. Eastwards these beds underlie the swelling moorlands of Pengwern and Welshmoor.

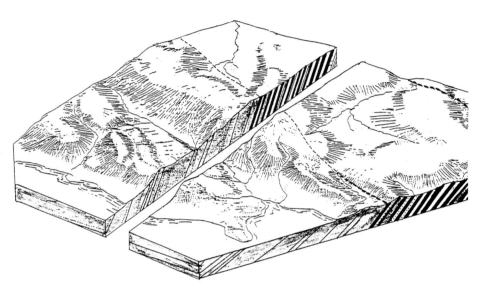

Heavy overlays of clay, mostly of glacial origin, are found throughout the parish and have considerable impact in impeding drainage. This results in extensive areas of poor, wet pasture land.

Coal measures - The coal measures of Llanrhidian consist of the Lower Coal Measures and the Pennant Series. The Lower Coal Measures contain the best coal seams in Wales and in Llanrhidian occur along the Morlais Valley eastwards towards Fairwood Common. The coal seams here, whilst of good quality , are much distorted and faulted making them difficult to exploit. Along the southern edge of the Morlais Valley they tend to be thin and stony (anthracitic) and of little commercial value. The scarp above the north side of the Morlais Valley marks the beginning of the Pennant Sandstones - hard, massive layers that make the bulk of the ridge running above Penclawdd towards Three Crosses. The Pennant beds were widely quarried for building materials all over north-east Gower.
It must be remembered that all these seams extend westward beneath the estuary and that the sands themselves have been excavated in the past so as to gain access to the coal seams.

Carboniferous Limestone - the free draining limestones have a marked influence on the landscape of the parish. Streams flowing off Cefn Bryn tend to disappear underground as they reach the limestone. Because of its chemical composition and the fact that it drains freely it makes the soils sweeter and improves farming. Thus the west end of the parish, where the limestone is found, has more arable and better pasture on enclosed fields. The limestone is exposed along the shore of the Burry estuary in a long line of old sea cliffs, now silted up, which have been extensively quarried. Limestone was used for building, fertiliser and for industrial processes. The close juxtaposition of limestones and coal seams in north Gower made the operation of limekilns economical.

Even for a parish as extensive as Llanrhidian the diversity of rocks outcropping across the area is remarkable; from the coal measures to the 350 million years old red sandstones. Between these are massive beds of Millstone Grit and Carboniferous Limestone. All these rocks dip under the Burry Estuary and re-emerge on the other side. Thus the ridge of Cefn Bryn along the south west boundary of the parish is echoed by the mountain ridge of the Carmarthen Fan 12 miles to the north.

Within the parish these rocks tend to dip at a steep angle towards the north but the trend or 'strike' of the outcrops is from just north of west to just south of east. At the east end of the parish the coal measures are severely broken by cracks or faults which make it almost impossible to follow any seam for more than a hundred yards.

Cilifor Top - formed by a hard sandstone band in the Millstone Grits.

Cefn Bryn - formed by an upward fold or 'anticline' of hard Old Red Sandstones.

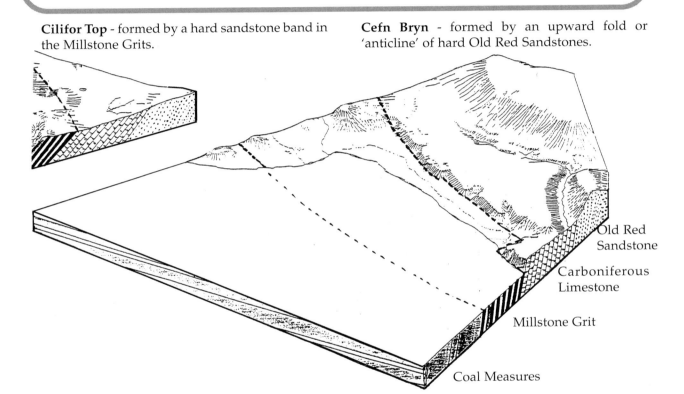

Old Red Sandstone

Carboniferous Limestone

Millstone Grit

Coal Measures

Old Red Sandstone - the massive red sandstones that form the Brecon Beacons and the Black Mountain a dozen miles to the north also give rise to Gower's highest hills and wildest moorlands, including Cefn Bryn. Within these beds are the hard and rugged conglomerates which were quarried and used for building and for making millstones. It is likely that most Gower millstones came from local beds of this material.

The moors of Cefn Bryn are extensively overlain by clays dating from the more recent glacial periods. These clays, which also overlay large areas of the limestones, impede drainage making the soil more acid and less productive.

Prehistoric Llanrhidian

Arthur's Stone

Arthur's Stone is, perhaps, Gower's best known landmark. It is a stone age burial chamber set on the northern crest of Cefn Bryn, slightly below the highest part of the ridge and overlooking the whole of Llanrhidian's parish. The position of the stone is not especially significant because the builders responsible appear to have exploited a massive boulder that was already in position. This boulder of quartz conglomerate is probably an 'erratic', shifted from its original site by an ice sheet in a glacial period. The neolithic builders of 5000 years ago, finding this spectacular boulder, excavated beneath it to create two burial chambers whilst inserting up to 12 upright stones to support it. The original boulder probably weighed above 35 tons but, as can be seen now, at least one major piece has come away. A large fragment lies beside the stone on the west side leaving the main boulder still weighing an estimated 25 tons. In the 17th century it was thought that some of the stone had been removed to make millstones but there is no corroborative evidence for this. The original site consisted of a large cairn some 23 metres across with stones possibly heaped up against the side of the capstone.

Traditions abound concerning the stone. The Arthurian connection is found in the story that Arthur, finding a pebble in his shoe, tossed it from Llanelli across the Burry estuary to land on Cefn Bryn. Other stories tell that the stone goes down to the Burry estuary each New year's Eve to sip the water and that the water, sometimes seen beneath the stone, rises and falls with the tide. The Welsh name,'Maen Ceti', has unknown derivation but dates back to at least the16th century when it was listed as one of the 'three mighty achievements of the Isle of Britain'. The name 'Ceti' is found in Sketty, a westerly suburb of Swansea. This is a contraction of 'Ynis Ceti', meaning 'Ceti's clearing'. The little stream that runs to the east of Penclawdd goes by the name of 'Cedi' (hence 'Abercedi' - the mouth of the Cedi) which could derive from the personal name.

Just to the east of Arthur's Stone some smaller stones have suggested to some observers an avenue of ritual significance but this is

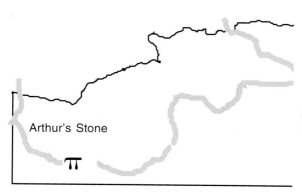

Arthur's Stone

Arthur's Stone from the south-west.

regarded as a tenuous possibility. Arthur's Stone is not the only structure of its type in Gower, others are to be found on the other side of Cefn Bryn near Nicholaston and on Rhossili Down. Not far from the parish boundary, in Green Cwm near Parkmill, is 'Giant's Grave' - one of the most sophisticated Stone Age tombs in Wales.

The Standing Stones of Llanrhidian

Where the people who built Arthur's Stone lived, we do not know; there is no direct evidence that the land that was to become Llanrhidian's parish was their home. But it is useful to speculate on the view they would have seen to the north of Cefn Bryn as they toiled around that great boulder. Probably, a sea of trees rolled up almost to the foot of the hill, oaks festooned with moss and lichen, alders growing out of wet swamps, tangled undergrowth in anything remotely like a clearing. These people would not have felt encouraged to choose this land, of all lands, out of the near empty wastes available to them. Where the limestone broke free of its clay covering, the trees were perhaps a little thinner, the clearings more negotiable. Thus it is not surprising that the first signs of humans within the parish area are to be found near its western limits.

Mansel Jack near Windmill Farm

These signs belong to what is now called the Bronze Age and are of two sorts. First, around the old megalith of Arthur's Stone and further along the ridge of Cefn Bryn, we find numerous burial places dated to that period of about 1800 BC to about 100BC. These burial places were cairns of various sizes, some nearly 20 metres across and bare of vegetation like the great cairn 100 metres west of Arthur's Stone. Most are much smaller and only visible to the trained eye. Arthur's Stone is at the north-west corner of a cairn field containing some 50 small stone cairns so overgrown as to be nearly invisible. Wherever the paths seem to be particularly strewn with small stones it is likely that a cairn is in the close vicinity. North of the ridge of Cefn Bryn and on the edge of the limestone area near Broad Pool the low barrow of Pen-y-crug represents an earthen essay in the same structure. One and a half miles west of Pen-y-crug we come to an interesting group of standing stones. Four survive, spread over a distance of less than a mile. Their purpose is unknown; they have been associated with funeral rites, waymarkers, ley lines and boundary posts but for certain, then as now, they mark the presence of Bronze Age man. Within the parish there are 4 stones still standing :-

The Ty'r Coed Stone

1. The Ty'r Coed Stone 2.5 metres high, incorporated into the hedge bank by the farm
2. Mansel Jack, an impressive monolith 3.2 metres high by the footpath from Manselfold Farm to Windmill Farm
3. Oldwalls Stone (1) in a hedge row just across the road from the Greyhound Inn, 1.5 metres high
4. Oldwalls Stone (2) in a hedge 2 fields west of the Greyhound Inn, standing 2.2 metres high.

The first two of these stones are found in fields called 'Stone Park' - the significance of the name is clear. This is a common occurrence throughout Gower where a further 4 stones are found (all around the western end of Cefn Bryn). The assumption is made that where this name 'Stone Field' occurs the presence of a former standing stone may be indicated. On this basis there may have been such a stone close to the western end of Welsh Moor and a further one above the Morlais Valley. In addition, the 2 stones standing on the green at Llanrhidian are of unknown origin and one of them may have been yet another Bronze Age monolith.

There are tantalising references in a manuscript of the early 18th century (*Badminton Court Book 2736*) to a 'great stone' on the hill above Penclawdd. This stone was to be replaced when water from an 'ancient fountain' called 'Ffynon Worgan' was diverted around Gwern Gored (Wern of the weir). A slightly later entry makes reference to 'Gwain Manheer' - was this meant to be 'menhir' or 'longstone'? An antiquarian of the following century (Lovett, *Welsh Pictures, 1892*) also mentioned a large stone that had recently stood in the vicinity. If there is significance in these references one would have to infer from the few clues they give that the stone stood somewhere between the crest of the hill (Graig Penclawdd) and the shore of the estuary to the north.

Broadly speaking, it appears that the Bronze Age peoples, who inhabited the land before the Celts, lived and farmed in the area of north-west Gower (although an early Bronze Age find has been made in the Dunvant area). Some small farms may have existed although no remains have survived. It is usual to associate the peoples of this era with a less settled 'slash and burn' approach to the land but this view is changing. Although some more permanent settlement may have existed, no remains have come to light. The general indication is that any settlement, permanent or transitory, was predominantly towards the west end of the parish.

The Bronze Age in Llanrhidian

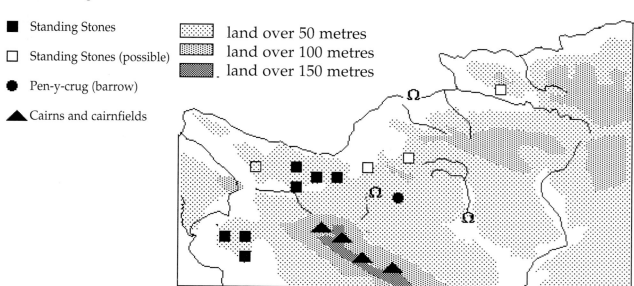

■ Standing Stones

□ Standing Stones (possible)

● Pen-y-crug (barrow)

▲ Cairns and cairnfields

land over 50 metres
land over 100 metres
land over 150 metres

The Celts Arrive

Traditionally seen as waves of artistic, warmongering Celts sweeping across the British Isles, the reality of Iron Age settlement is likely to have been far more prosaic. The so called 'Bronze Age peoples' were very likely established in the western part of Llanrhidian in the centuries before Christ; the arriving Celts may have found them practising crude agriculture and pastoralism from some small settlement around the western end of Cefn Bryn. No evidence survives of such a settlement which may have been far from permanent. The Iron Age Celts who first entered the area probably came by sea from across the Bristol channel or even directly from north west France. The number of people already settled in the Gower peninsula would have been very small. With room for all there would have been little cause for conflict; coexistence and intermarriage may well have been common practice.

The typical settlement pattern of these newcomers is reflected in their hilltop and promontory forts. These forts are common in Gower along the coasts and on Llanmadoc Hill. In the Llanrhidian area there are at least six earthworks from the period all of which appear to have had a defensive purpose. Each 'fort' was probably the focal point of a local farming community, the centre of an agricultural estate owned by Celtic aristocrats or their underlings. At their disposal were the forests that still clothed the greater part of north Gower, the grasslands of the highest parts and the farmlands established by their predecessors or by their own clearances. Such farmlands were on the best drained slopes and lowlands available.

Bronze Brooch c100AD from the Bishopston Valley Swansea Museum (Royal Institution of South Wales)

The largest of these forts was Cilifor on the great brooding hilltop just east of Llanrhidian; it is among the largest and most impressive settlements of its kind in south Wales. Its size suggests that it was pre-eminent in north Gower, probably in all of Gower. Officially described as a multivallate defensive structure it can be seen that there were two or three lines of defensive ditches and banks around it except on the east where a spectacular drop makes them unnecessary. The enclosed area is 2.9 hectares. Within the defences, nearer the northern end, up to six hut platforms have been detected. The main entrance was probably towards the north-west side where a terraced road way appears to approach the defences.

Other earthworks in the area are much smaller. Described by the Royal Commission as the 'Stembridge Hillfort', the little promontory earthwork above a stream near Fairyhill stands outpost at the extreme west end of the parish. Its original name may well have been 'Pen Cynas', the name of the adjacent field. The reason for this supposition will become apparent later but is significant and the name Pencynas will be used in future references to the site in this text. It stands on a little promontory of land standing steeply above the Redwell Lake stream and required defences only to isolate the promontory from more level land to the north east where a hefty bank and ditch with a smaller outer bank stand guard. The enclosed area is only one fifth of a hectare.

Penannular Bronze Brooch – Iron Age c400AD from Whiteford Burrows Swansea Museum (Royal Institution of South Wales)

Towards the other end of the parish a number of small univallate (single line of defence) earthworks are to be found. The chief of these is Pen y Gaer, above present day Penclawdd, 0.9 hectare in area. Here again the steep natural slopes on the north and south make defensive banks necessary only on the east and west sides. At other points on the long ridge leading from here to Three Crosses there are signs of early settlement, particularly at Gron Gaer just east of Llanyrnewydd Church. Here a tiny enclosure of 0.1 hectare stands partially defended above a steep defile to its west. On the northern flanks of the ridge, hanging above the marshes of the Burry Estuary, stands the equally tiny site of Hen Gastell above Abercedi. Here a single bank 'defends' the enclosure on its landward side. On the ridge east of Penygaer a number of field shapes have rounded edges suggestive of other possible enclosures - it is highly likely that this ridge above the village of Penclawdd was well populated at the beginning of the first millennium AD and has known continuous population in some form ever since.

Also to be noted is the earthwork near Cilonnen, hidden amongst trees but sited above a steep slope down into the Morlais valley. There is yet another possible site a half kilometre to the west around an old farm ruin and both may relate to a medieval estate of the pre-Norman period with their roots in the earlier Celtic period.

It is notable that these prehistoric earthworks manage to retain Welsh names. This may not be thought surprising in the Welsh half of the area but across 'English' Gower the old places still have Welsh names attached. These may have survived only in field names as at the old hill fort in Rhossili (Caer Ditch) or in adjacent properties like Penmynnydd by the 'Bulwark' camp on Llanmadoc Hill. In 'English' Llanrhidian the field name 'Pencynas' survives in a sea of English names and Cilifor is an anomaly amongst the English names used around it. It is likely that these names came from the period before Anglicisation took place in much of the peninsula and as such they may be close to the original names given them by their Celtic creators.

Celtic settlements in Llanrhidian

land over 50 metres

land over 100 metres

land over 150 metres

Iron age earthwork - size indicated by size of marker

Our Celtic ancestors, esconced in Pen y gaer on the ridge above Penclawdd, would have looked down and across the estuary to see smoke rising from the little Roman settlement of Leucarum or Loughor. Although the Silures, to which tribe the Gower inhabitants probably belonged, put up a stiff initial resistance to the Romans it seems that for most of the period of Roman occupation there was little conflict. It is possible that there were one or two Roman estates in west Gower, certainly there was a villa on the south side of Swansea Bay. Therefore, the sight of Roman people or their representatives making their way along the ridgeways of north Gower might not have been uncommon.

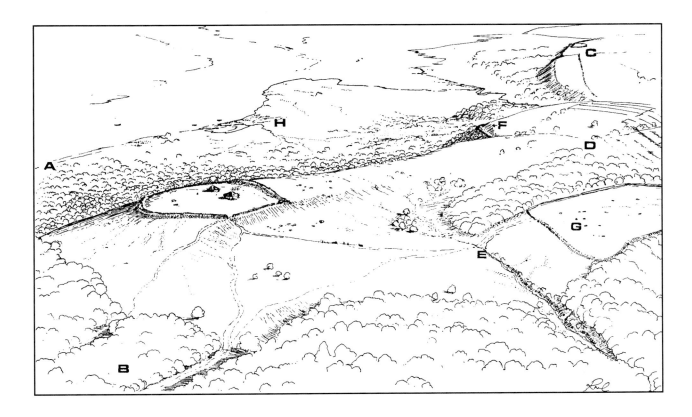

Penygaer as it may have appeared when viewed from the south west, 2000 years ago. Note the following:

A   - the site of present day 'Tabernacle' in Penclawdd
B   - the site of the now ruined 'Hermon' Chapel
C   - Hen Gastell, an Iron Age enclosure above Aberdedi
D   - the site of Llotrog
E   - the site of Dwrllais at the head of a stream running to the Morlais
F   - the ditch running eastwards from Penygaer from Penclawdd may have derived its name
H   - the site of today's Health Centre

Indeed, it is possible that more suspicion may have been reserved for people of the Demetae tribe, the forerunners of the kingdom of Dyfed. It is not entirely clear where the boundary between the Silures and the Demetae lay but, for certain, Gower was in the border zone between the two and, when the Romans departed, the area was subject to dispute and conflict.

Reference - *'An Inventory of the Ancient Monuments in Glamorgan, Vol.1'* HMSO 1976

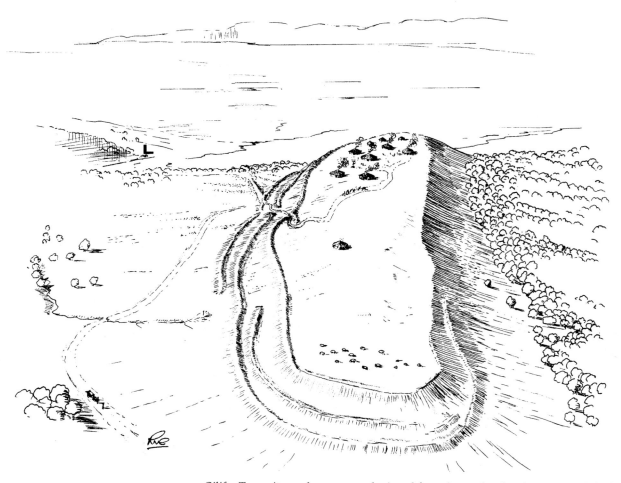

Cilifor Top as it may have appeared, viewed from the south, when it was occupied. The steep hill slope to the east made earthworks unnecessary on that side. The entrance was from the Llanrhidian village side and it is likely that the principal farmlands of the occupying group lay in that direction. Such hillforts as this were probably used in times when defensive measures were thought necessary rather than as permanent settlements. 'L' marks the site of the present day Llanrhidian village.

Medieval Llanrhidian

With the departure of the Romans the local tribes were more or less free to choose their own destinies as much as it lay in their power. For a time it would appear that the region of the Gower peninsula was a kingdom in its own right. During the fifth and sixth centuries documentary evidence suggests that this was the case but that the peninsula later became part of the burgeoning kingdom of Glywysing - the dominant state of south Wales and roughly commensurate with the old county of Glamorgan. Glywysing may well have been the later political expression of the old tribe of the Silures. Gower would have represented the western march of Glywysing, bordering on the powerful kingdom of Dyfed. Dyfed was probably the same state as that of the old rival tribe of the Demetae but had also gone through a period of very extensive Irish influence. Unfortunately for the people of our region, Gower became the object of territorial ambition and changed hands between the competing kingdoms more than once. At the same time, other pressures were being felt in the region as Danish attacks took place along the coast and settlements were made by them, notably at Swansea in the tenth century. It is hard to imagine that the peninsula had developed up to this time without the influence of this major centre but henceforth it would come to dominate the economic activity of the region, its politics, settlement patterns and road networks. There is no direct evidence that in the later part of this period, before the Norman invasion, English settlers were arriving in Gower but this has often been supposed to be the case. One may summarise this period of the history of Llanrhidian by saying that it experienced some periods of relative peace but became increasingly pressured by the ambitions of regional kingdoms, Danish and (possibly) English settlers.

Contemporary accounts describe south Wales as a land of impenetrable forests, bogs and marshes. Valley sides, where not cloaked in woodland were covered in thorn and thistle, flatter lands with thickets of reeds and thornbushes. The period after the Romans experienced a climatic decline. The weather was cooler and wetter but towards the end of the first millenium conditions were beginning to improve. With a very limited population it must have been difficult to establish control of the land and to make it productive.

There has been much discussion of the manner in which people controlled and worked the land in Wales and it is very tempting to try and discern patterns in any given area. For example, a basic settlement pattern was the 'gwely', a family holding of upwards of 40 acres. Such properties were sub-divided between members of the family through successive generations with farms being established around the ancestral land or hiving-off to new pastures. Such a 'gwely' has been discerned in the farm and field patterns of Dunvant before it was covered in extensive estate building. Just a mile or so to the west similar patterns exist at Cilonnen or to the north of Three Crosses but there is almost no evidence to corroborate the existence of such holdings at that time. It is, therefore, essential to examine the little historical evidence there is for settlement in Llanrhidian during this crucial and formative period. Two documentary

The Leper Stone in Llanrhidian Church porch where it rests in a horizontal position. About 2 metres long, it may have been part of a lintel block in a building in the pre-Norman period. The representations appear to be of human figures together with design motifs, possibly of an animalistic nature.

sources exist that can help us. The first is the 'Brut y Tywysogion', the annals of early Welsh history, that makes some general references to Llanrhidian particularly in the year 1099 when the Normans built a castle there. This confirms the existence of a Welsh settlement predating the arrival of the Normans. The Leper Stone, now in the porch of Llanrhidian Church confirms that some settlement existed there in the ninth or tenth centuries. Recently interpreted as a Viking gravestone, this stone with its animalistic and crude carving is among the most enigmatic of Gower's ancient remains. On the green at Llanrhidian stand two stones one of which has been interpreted as a damaged cross, again dating from the pre-Norman period. Together, this evidence indicates the existence of a settlement at Llanrhidian during, and possibly before, the ninth century. The name 'Llanrhidian' is also an indicator of early date. It implies an enclosure made, in this instance, for religious purposes and connected with the somewhat obscure figure of Rhidian. The prefixing of the word 'llan' (enclosure) to a personal name is typical of places with religious connections dating back to the period of the early Welsh kingdoms. Llanelen would appear to have been a small but active religious community, just to the west of Llanrhidian, possibly as early as the 6th or 7th century. Another 'llan' name, originally connected with a personal name 'Gwynour' was the probable origin of the name Llanyrnewydd, a chapel of unknown provenance serving as the church to present day Penclawdd. First mentioned in the Tudor period it may have origins in a much earlier era.

The second documentary source for the period, the 'Book of Llandaff', makes reference to a 'Lan Pencreig' in a charter dealing with properties during the seventh century. It is widely accepted that this relates to Pen-y-craig above Penclawdd. Unfortunately, the interpretation of 'Lan Conuur' in the same document as referring to Llangwynour is not now accepted as it was last century. It is worth mentioning, in spite of scholarly opinion, that the name 'Conor' occurs in the nearby stream of Nant Conor (a name found in an 18th century document) which flows through the farmyard of Cwm Cynnar. This same charter, 144 in Wendy Davies's notation of the Liber Landavensis, refers to Lan Cyngualan which, although firmly located elsewhere, contains the element 'cyngu' found in the adjacent but now lost farm of 'Kyngy' near Crofty.

One further item of evidence, this time archaeological, may relate to this early period of Llanrhidian's history. The Celtic earthwork of Cilifor has a small 'ringwork' inserted into the south-east end of its summit. The Royal Commission interpreted this as a medieval insertion. It would certainly suggest that the old hill fort was re-used, if in a very limited way, at some time during the period in question and it may even have been regarded as Llanrhidian's castle.

In the period just before the Normans began to make their influence felt, it is likely that most of the Gower peninsula, outside of the growing settlement of Swansea, belonged to some political unit. The area of north Gower in which Llanrhidian is central belonged to what was later to become the manor of Landimore. This manor may have been a relic of a traditional Welsh 'maenor' comprising a number of townships of which Llanrhidian itself would have been one. Even after the Normans had

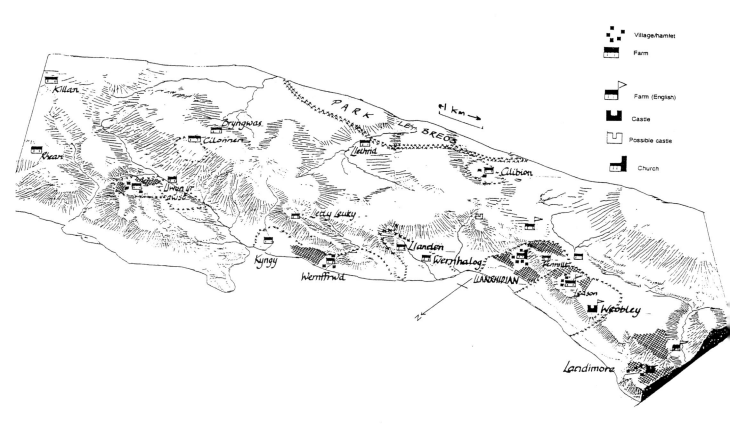

Medieval Llanrhidian - showing Welsh and Anglo/Norman settlements across the parish

The two stones on the green at Llanrhidian are of ancient origin, the higher of them being possibly the remains of a medieval cross. It was reputedly used as a pillory in the last century. An annual fair was held on the green at Llanrhidian in the last century, this too may have had much earlier origins.

carved up the manor, Landimore still had lands comprising all of Rhossili, Cheriton and the greater part of Llanrhidian. It is not at all unreasonable to suppose that the manor, prior to the Normans, also included Llangennith, Llanmadoc and possibly Llanddewi at the very least. The chief place of this substantial manor may well have been Landimore itself but more imposing settlements such as Llangennith, sometimes called the 'capital' of Gower, or even Llanrhidian appear to have longer histories and possibly better claims.

The Normans Arrive

The Normans arrived in Gower around the year 1095, some 30 years after their victory at Hastings. They first established a stronghold in Swansea but within four years, so the annals tell us, they built a castle at Llanrhidian. The site of this castle is not known - it may have been the inserted ringwork on Cilifor's old hill fort, it may have been sited above the old village church in the area now completely altered by later lime quarries. Whatever the site, the Normans had an immediate need to assert control over the area. In the western part of the parish that was to become so anglicised the existing hamlets and villages that had to be controlled can be discerned by the survival of Welsh names. Llanrhidian itself, Cillibion, Llethrid and Llanelen were settlements already established. Farms such as Penrhallt above Llanrhidian and Llwyn-y-bwch may also have been established. Further east, where the English tongue did not assert itself in the form of place-names, it is harder to detect previously established Welsh settlements but a series of grants made by William de Breos in 1315 have survived which name some, at least, of the farms and communities. Evidence has already led us to expect that Cilonnen was a possible 'gwely' from the old times and its existence is confirmed by these grants. Arable land was held here and close to Bryngwas by William ap Richard; nearby Rees ap Llewellyn held meadow and arable lands at Gellihir and Rhean.

Farms also existed at Killan and Llwyn-yr-awst (deep in the Morlais valley). These seem to have been mostly holdings in the hands of single family groups; a typical pattern of Welsh settlement would show such a scatter of freehold farmers spread across the landscape. But at Wernffrwd a different pattern is apparent where de Breos granted Robert of Penrice small portions of arable and meadow land interspersed with the lands of numerous Welshmen - Adam son of Griffith ap Jeruart, Llewellyn ap Cadwgan, Philip ap Griffith ap Jeruart and others. So small are the amounts of land, and so interspersed, we have to conclude that some are narrow strips in larger fields which were worked communally. This is a different pattern of settlement, doubtless existing also at Llanrhidian, where the villagers were not freeholders and worked the land together.

Robert of Penrice, as a knight, was one of the beneficiaries of the Norman occupation. In return for his military service to de Breos, the local marcher lord, he was granted ownership of land. Such grants became known as 'Knights fees' and were controlled as manors. It would appear that the power of the old manor of Landimore was broken up early on by such grants. The manor of Weobley was established on what was probably unfarmed land but separating Landimore from its eastern

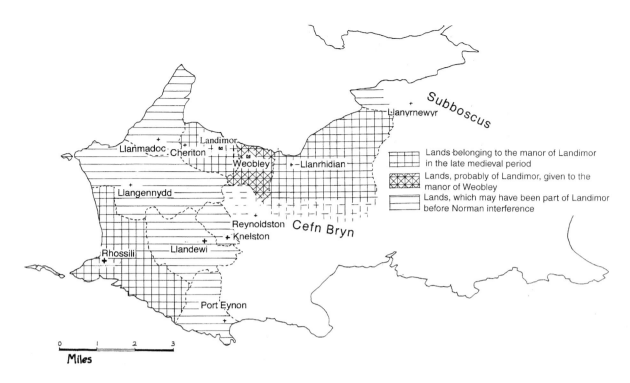

Lands belonging to the manor of Landimor in the late medieval period

Lands, probably of Landimor, given to the manor of Weobley

Lands, which may have been part of Landimor before Norman interference

lands of Llanrhidian. To the west the district of Llangennith was granted to the abbey of St Evreux in France, thus separating Landimore from its south eastern lands at Rhossili. The manor was thus, effectively, emasculated.

New farms were established in the western part of Llanrhidian, revealed by their suffix of '-ton', the old Saxon indicator of a farm. A personal name before might indicate the first owner's name as at Leisonston, later to become shortened to Leason, or Walterston on the southern edge of the parish. Leason was acquired by the Normans in the 13th century and was in the hands of David de la Bere by 1304 as a military tenure. De la Bere was instrumental in the building of Weobley Castle and the inhabitants of the adjacent hamlet of Leason were surely employed by him.

Weobley Castle

Weobley Castle stands on a dramatic site at the extreme western edge of the parish of Llanrhidian. On the crest of a very steep slope, it overlooks the vast sands and marshes of the Burry Estuary to the north. To the east it looks towards Penclawdd, three miles away across the marsh edge. Closer to hand on the west is the hamlet of Landimore, originally the heart of a Welsh manor, where the villagers would have been painfully aware of this assertion of Norman authority over lands that once belonged to them.

Weobley is easily the best known and most picturesque of Llanrhidian's medieval remains. It was the main building of one of the knights' fees that were distributed amongst the Norman elite in Swansea and Gower in 1106. This was well before the Welsh had lost their long

The possible extent of the manor of Landimore in the days before the Norman invasion of Wales

The de la Bere tomb in Stretford, near Weobley in Herefordshire, displaying the family arms (see over).

17

Weobley Castle viewed from the east.
The polygonal turret nearest was used mainly as
an elaborate garderobe or latrine.

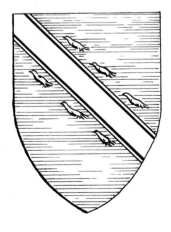

The De la Bere arms - bore, azure,
a bend cotised argent between six
martlets or

struggle for independence. Any Gower holding outside Swansea, prior to 1282 (the death of the last Llewelyn) might be regarded as nominal. Indeed, the evidence available suggests that it was not until after 1282 that the castle was begun. Although it is cited as an example of a fortified manor house, the initial works included the south-west tower which was a small castle-like keep with massively thick walls. For more than a hundred years local and national revolts would spring up and this defensive strength was probably needed. At about the same time, according to the evidence of the buildings, the northern domestic block (hall and kitchen) and the eastern curtain wall were completed. This work was probably completed under the eye of David de la Bere, the first name associated with the castle. The de la Beres had a connection with Weobley in Herefordshire that must have pre-dated the foundation of the castle. The details of this connection are not known but it persisted into the 15th century and must have accounted for the name of the Gower manor and castle. By about 1320 the main building programme was complete with the western curtain wall, gatehouse, solar block, chapel, eastern domestic block and the large hexagonal garderobe tower. But before that something must have caused the de la Beres to limit their ambitions for the castle; there is clear evidence that a more extensive wall to the west was never completed, nor was a strong tower on the south-east corner for which massive foundations were laid. The castle remained, however, in the hands of the de la Beres for more than a century although very severely damaged in the Glyndwr rebellion according to a report of 1410.

Little change took place until Weobley was acquired, probably through family connections, by the rising star of the new Tudor period - Sir Rhys ap Thomas. To make the building more suited to his wealth and status he added the porch block. This gave a more genteel entrance to the domestic apartments. The execution of Rhys's grandson, for treason, in 1531 led to the castle becoming crown property. The demesne lands were now being farmed by a tenant farmer probably using the castle as his farmhouse. Some adjustments to the internal structure were made at this time so that the building, now presumably becoming somewhat delapidated, could be used as a farmhouse. The property was sold to the Earl of Pembroke, Sir William Herbert, but after another century had passed it finally came into the hands of the Margam estate. By this time the castle was entirely disused and 'decayed'. The demesne lands of the castle were worked from a new farmhouse adjacent to the ruins by tenant farmers such as William Seys who, in 1665, held

> *'All that decayed castle called Wibley Castle with the site thereof and barn consisting of five bayes adioyninge to the sd castle and one cowhouse...one ffarmehouse barn and cowhouse' (1665 Survey of Weobley)*

Today the castle remains one of the better preserved fortified dwellings to be found in Wales. Visitors entering through the main gatehouse should bear in mind that all the principal rooms were on the first floor at the height of the wooden gallery provided in the main hall. The main hall, the solar, the chapel and tower (to the right) would all have looked down into the small enclosed courtyard. This courtyard, without Rhys ap Thomas's porch, would have been a somewhat more spacious area during the first 150 years of the castle's life. Visitors would be well advised to use the excellent guide provided by 'Cadw' or to consult with the original HMSO guide by W G Thomas to which this account is much indebted.

Llanrhidian Church

Llanrhidian Church is the oldest building remaining in the parish and, as such, it is remarkable that it is still in regular use. The present structure dates largely from the 13th century but clearly there was a church of some sort on or near this site for long before that. References in the Welsh annals occur from 1099 onwards; as we have seen, where the prefix 'llan' occurs with the personal name of a saint a religious enclosure is clearly implied. The mysterious 'Rhidian' would have lived well before the 11th century, the traditional foundation of the church is in the 6th century. In 1185 the Margam annals record

> *' a certain thing wonderful by its novelty occurred.. about the feast of the nativity of St John the Baptist.... in a village called Llanrhidian, and on the fifth day of the week. Instead of spring water, a copious stream of milk flowed constantly for three hours from a certain well which the inhabitants call St Illtyd's Well. Many who were present testified that while they were looking at the milk stream attentively and with astonishment, they also saw among the gravel lying about in every direction, and all around the edge of the well, a certain fatty substance*

Weobley Castle - the main entrance from the west

19

Llanrhidian Church tower, the oldest complete part of the building dating from the 13th century - probably built by the Knights Hospitallers of St John of Jerusalem.

floating about, such as is collected from milk, and from which butter is made'.

This well is now identified as one that still bubbles up in a garden at the lower end of the main village street. The dedication of the well to St Illtyd is the same as the present dedication of the church.

In 1167, or thereabouts, the church was given by the lord of the manor of Landimore, William Turberville, to the Knights Hospitallers of St John of Jerusalem. This order, with its headquarters at Slebech in Pembrokeshire, acquired much property in Gower at this time including the other Landimore churches of Rhossili and Landimore (Cheriton). Since the building style of the surviving medieval parts of the church is consistent with that of the 13th century we must credit the Knights with the construction of the present church. At the west end is the solid tower, of obvious defensive qualities and equipped with a stone fire beacon - indicators of the turbulent times in which it was built. The long nave was completely rebuilt in 1856 but the original dimensions were maintained. The chancel is a fairly complete survival from the original 13th century building. In 1400 the Knights were reproached by the Bishop of St Davids for 'it was found that the chancel ..... was in ruins and notoriously in want of rebuilding'. Local parishioners, David Gogh, David Wylly, Nicholas ap Traharn and John Oweyn were employed to repair it; we may attribute some of the fabric of the chancel to the work of these men although the east window is a late insertion. Apart from the rebuilding of 1856-58 the only other known restoration was carried out between 1899 and 1901.

Llanelen

There are more stories surrounding Llanelen than any other site in Llanrhidian. These stem from the fact that it has always been thought that this was the site of an old church dating from the the first millenium. Together with this have grown stories of a lost village, abandoned in the Black Death and of mysterious connections with the Arthurian legend. Recent excavations have let new light shine on this fascinating site and revealed valuable details of life contemporary with the building of Llanrhidian Church and prior to Weobley Castle.

Between 1318 and 1327 grants of land to Robert de Penres and Thomas Day of about 8 acres were made at Llanelen, we may safely assume that these were farmlands. The present Llanelen Farm is high on the ridge above a caravan site but the original settlement was a quarter of a mile to the west on the south facing slope of the ridge.

Excavations revealed the old church, a tiny affair which began as a wooden structure just 2 metres wide and 3 metres long in the 6th or 7th centuries. It seems likely that this church was sequestrated in the 13th century and the excavations confirmed that by this time the building was not in ecclesiastical use. The material finds of the excavations belonged largely to the period between the discontinuation of the use of the church and the final abandonment of the site in the mid 14th century. These revealed that the decaying chapel building was used, for possibly a further 100 years or more after the cessation of religious activity, as a farming homestead with a very mixed economy. Barley and oats were grown, quite possibly sown together in a mixture called 'drage'. The discovery of a stone quern for milling corn showed that these crops were processed on the farm. Bones of sheep and cattle suggested the probable livestock holding. Finds of cockle shells showed that the estuary was part of the resources for people living at Llanelen. A long hedge boundary around Llanelen indicates that a holding of some 80 acres sustained the farm but there was also access to the pastures of Welsh Moor to the south and to the marshes north and west. Much of the 80 acres may have been woodland, another useful resource in the light of the finds of iron working on the site. Iron ores might have been found in the lower coal measures just north of Llanelen or in the limestone/millstone grit boundary to the south. A number of locations in the close vicinity of Llanelen indicate that iron was smelted nearby. It seems that 'furnaces' were set up in clearings around the farm. Cooking vessels dating from c1250 to 1350 were found, probably of local origin. Glazed ware was also

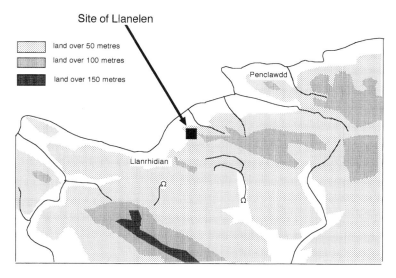

A reconstruction of Llanelen Chapel as it may have looked about 1200. The photograph shows the site as it looks today.

found originating from the west of England and France. The French ware probably contained wine, a surprising luxury in this obscure corner of medieval Gower. Whilst the farmer may have survived on the produce of his farm the profits from the simple iron production may have paid for such luxuries.

The fact that the site was abandoned at roughly the same time as the Black Death gives credence to the local tradition that a village here was destroyed by the plague. It is always dangerous to draw general conclusions from specific instances but we might be justified, in the absence of other evidence, in supposing that Llanellen could be a model for other, contemporaneous, farms in the area. Cilonnen, Cefn Bychan, Wernffrwd may all have worked on the same mixed economy, using the varied food and mineral resources of the area. In later years the whole area was to be distinguished by this very trait.

This account draws heavily on an account by Schlesinger, Walls etc in the Gower Magazine (46). The author is also much indebted to Dr. Jonathan Kissock's assistance and learned interpretations of the Gower landscape .

Welsh and English - the first divide

A glance at the modern map of Gower clearly indicates, from the place names alone, the areas dominated by Welsh and English cultures. Today, the extent of the English dominance in Gower appears far greater than it was around 1400 after the Norman/English settlers had first established themselves. A line drawn through the parish from Llanrhidian to Cillibion and on to Llethrid farm would have marked the western limit of the Welsh dominated part of the parish. South and west of this line were the new settlements like Leason, Walterston and Weobley. East of this boundary non-Welsh settlers found themselves surrounded by native, and probably not very welcoming, Welsh. The whole of the Gower peninsula in the days before the conquest belonged to the lower division of the commote of Gower and would have been known as 'Gwyr Iscoed' - Gower below the wood. Anglicised, the peninsula was known

English and Welsh elements in pre-nineteenth century place names in the parish of Llanrhidian.

++++   *Western limit of Welsh language c1700*
-----   *Lower/higher parish division*
●   *Welsh place name*
○   *English place name*
Double rings signify chief settlements

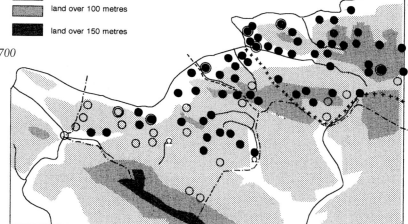

land over 50 metres
land over 100 metres
land over 150 metres

to the settlers as 'Gower Anglicana' - English Gower. But this could not apply to those Welsh people in the north-east of the peninsula who still regarded themselves as part of Iscoed, translated into Latin as 'Subboscus'. It was always difficult to know the boundary between Welsh and English Gower but the name 'Welsh Moor' surely dates from this early period when it was the only large common in the 'Welshry'. Although subject to the overlordship of the Normans from their castle in Swansea, these inhabitants of Subboscus lived according to the Welsh traditions and had their rents and taxes collected in the old way. But, being part of the manor of Subboscus, they found their lives increasingly under the sway of the growing town of Swansea. Nonetheless, the traditional pattern of settlement was continued. It was not in the Welsh tradition to form villages when a man could establish himself on his own stretch of land. At Wernffrwd, as we have seen ('*The Normans Arrive*') there were indications of traditions of communal farming, it is likely that something of the same sort was already established in Llanrhidian. At Leason, on the other hand, the pattern of strip fields was clearly established in the fashion of the settlers. It was a system by which any single farmer would have his lands, mostly furlong strips, distributed across the township or communally owned lands. He would expect to have a strip in most fields, often more than one strip in a field. Villages such as Llanrhidian and Leason consisted of farming homesteads gathered around the main street or church. Vestiges of this system still survive in Gower, notably at Rhossili but, by 1400, the system was already in decline.

War, Famine and Pestilence

The medieval period, at its close, was a time of difficulty and suffering for people all across Europe. Wales had more than its fair share of this and Llanrhidian was clearly affected by the triple scourge of war, famine and plague.

From the first arrival of the Normans in south Wales, about 1100, to the pacification of 1282 and beyond, there was little peace in the country. Again and again the Welsh tried to reassert their control over Gower. Between 1200 and 1230 the manor of Landimore was in the gift of Llewellyn the Great. Gower was the scene of fighting in 1215 , 1217, and, after the defeat of the last Llewellyn, in 1287. Further uprisings took place during the early part of the 14th century and these coincided with the most unpropitious conditions for farming in generations. From 1314 to 1321 crops were devastated by successive summers of heavy rain, there being an intermission of drought in one year. Typhoid broke out in 1316, whilst sheep and cattle were severely afflicted by disease, probably connected with the adverse weather conditions. Outbreaks of unrest at this time were unlikely to have been welcomed by a peasantry struggling to survive against the odds.

It is against this background that the Black Death struck Britain in 1348. Although details of its progress in Gower are not known, evidence of its effects in our area are to be found. The main effect of the Black death was the loss of a very significant proportion of the population. Fields would become untended, farms vacant and food prices unstable as a result. The effects were long lasting so, although nearly half a century had elapsed, the country had not recovered when Owain Glyndwr made a last bid for Welsh independence. Gower was in no way spared the effects of the devastation that followed and in less than a century had been ravaged by war, famine and pestilence.

That Llanrhidian was severely affected by this disastrous century is evidenced in a number of ways. In 1369, after years of ruined crops, disease and plague, the manor of Landimore was 'farmed'. This was a device by which the local inhabitants or outside parties could buy or rent their way into the estate so that income could still be derived by the lord of the manor. This was particularly important to him if he had lost the manpower to work his lands for his own advantage. In spite of this, much of the land of the manor remained empty and some farms and lands fell into complete disuse. This was doubtless the case at Llanelen which was abandoned about this time.

The fact that Weobley Castle was badly damaged in the course of the Glyndwr rebellion surely reflects more widespread damage in the area. For example, at the same time we find the chancel of Llanrhidian church in such a sorry state that it could not be used. On the basis of this circumstantial evidence we can begin to imagine what was happening to the community and the lands it had painstakingly won from the woods and marshes. Farms such as Llwyn yr Awst may, like Llanelen, have been abandoned at this time. Others, such as Cilwascruallan and Llwynycho (names and spellings deduced from a 1328 manuscript) are now unknown to us and may have gone the same way. These were all individual holdings scattered about the 'Welsh' end of the parish. In such places the death of a farmer may have led to the abandonment of a whole farm. At the other end of the parish, where communally worked fields were more common, the death of individuals had a different effect on the land. The immediate result would have been that the deceased farmer's strips in the common field would have run to waste. This would have been most undesirable to neighbouring strip holders who would have sought to bring those waste strips into their own holding. Within a few years the complex patchwork of strips would have become more like a number of rectangular fields within a common field. From this stage it is but a small step to the pattern we see today of these same rectangular fields with hedges grown around them. Hedge dating suggests that this last process may have taken place around 1500 to 1650. In this sense we can see that the marks of the terrible 14th century are still with us in the field patterns.

Leason

Leason was probably founded as a medieval settlement providing manpower for the castle and manor of Weobley just to the west. Leason, or Leisonston as it was then known, was the only settlement in that part of the manor. As has been shown, the Black Death and the vicissitudes of the 14th century probably did much to undermine the economy of the area and the old common fields began to be broken up and consolidated. By the middle 1700's little was left of the old medieval settlement and

Medieval farmer sowing - wall painting in Easby church - N Yorks.

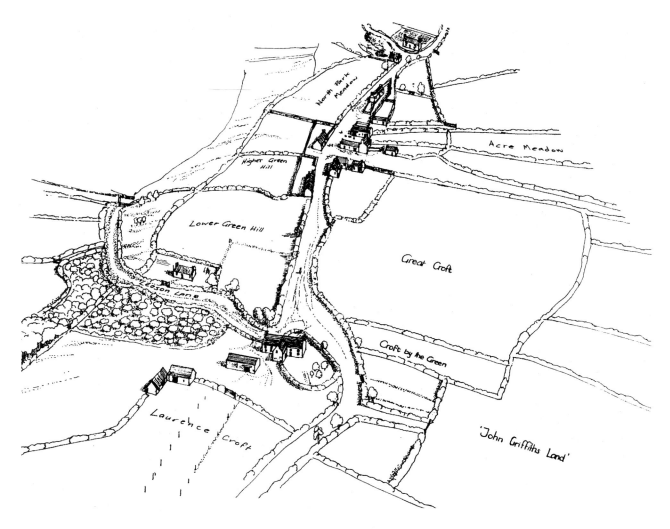

new buildings were replacing older ones. The old track that led along the crest of the escarpment above the marsh was still a central thoroughfare but the lane to Oldwalls was the quickest way to the Swansea road. Leason Lane, in the foreground, gave vital access to the marsh for sheep. It descended the steep slope to Leason Well, before leading straight out to the marsh. At the other end of the village Lodgecott Lane led down to a sheepfold and also gave access to the marsh and meadows below the hill.

Reconstruction of Leason as it looked c1800. Oldwalls and the Greyhound Inn are about a quarter mile to the right of this scene, the marsh is off to the left.

The development of Leason fields from medieval times

Hedge surveys in the Leason area (assessing the age of the hedge by measuring its variety of woody plants) indicate that this interpretation of the developments is broadly correct. Species counts range from 2 to 5 per 30 metres with a predominance of hawthorn, blackthorn and elder. This could be taken to suggest enclosure of strips taking place continuously from the early Tudor period. Among the oldest hedgerows is that on the east side of the lane leading to Leason from the south. This suggests that the first act of enclosure would have been to separate the east and west fields by taking the east field into private hands.

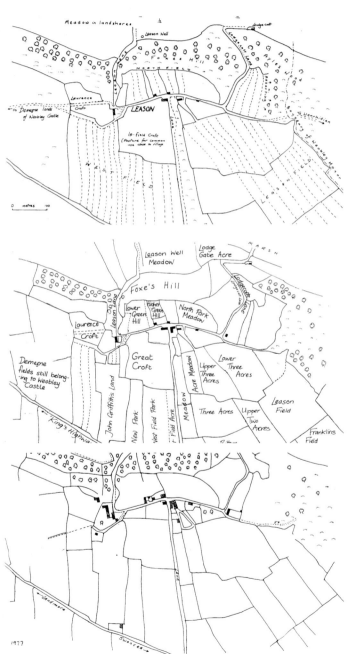

1. Conjectural reconstruction of how the fields looked, with their strips, prior to the Black Death etc.. Each farmer, includingthe Lord of the Manor in nearby Weobley Castle, would have worked strips in each field.

2. In 1785 some of the strips still survived but in a greatly altered form. Most of the strip had long been 'consolidated' into long rectangular fields.

3. By 1977 all the strips had disappeared but to the discerning eye the evidence of their existence is there to be seen.

26

A New Era

Emerging from the nightmare of the 14th century and the Glyndwr rebellion, north Gower could look forward to a period of slow rebuilding. For a number of reasons it could never be called prosperous and even today is looked upon by many as a poor neighbour to south Gower.

As early as 1400, the bailiff's returns for the manor of Landimore reveal that marginal lands were being enclosed, particularly around the edge of the estuary marshes. Throughout the manor, which even then extended almost the whole length of the Burry estuary, enclosures such as *'pasture of Westimerche'*, *'2 acres of land and salt meadow at Lanridean'*, *'3 acres of meadow near Landymore in the Marchemede'* are found in the returns. Clearly the prime land was already taken and the value of the marshes was becoming apparent. Recent studies have revealed that at this time the inhabitants were beginning to look inland at areas that were previously thought intractable. New farms were also springing up from lands that were once worked in common by the villagers. Penrallt, adjacent to Llanrhidian, was in the private hands of Hoskin Thomas by 1472 and private lands flanked his fields. The carving out of new farms from wood and moorland was also common. Typical of such ventures must have been Wernhalog, almost certainly an upshot from the decayed settlement at Llanelen and possibly established within a generation of the demise of that ancient settlement.

The Tudor period brought new opportunities and fresh impetus to expansion. There is, unfortunately, a great dearth of documentary evidence relating to settlements in the 15th century. As a result we may be tempted to argue from lack of evidence that many new farms were not established until late Tudor times of which records are more informative. It would seem wisest, however, to describe the parish at the time of Queen Elizabeth I with the assumption that many of the farms then operating may have been working for a century or more.

Along the coastal margin we find farms at Staffal Haegr, Wernhalog, Aberlogin, Kingie (near Cwm Cynnar), Llanmorlais, Crofty, Pencaerfenni, Abercedi and Berthlwyd. Penclawdd Issaf was probably also such a farm - somewhere in the vicinity of today's Tabernacle Chapel. The better draining ridges also sustained a number of settlements, in particular the ridge above Penclawdd and leading up towards what would be 'Three Crosses'. Cefnbychan was an historic settlement to the south of the ridge, Penylan a rather newer one on a level platform halfway up the northern slopes of 'Graig Penclawdd'. Further inland were farms at Hendy, Crwys, Killan and Wimblewood. Above the Morlais valley, too, there were farms on the Wern and at (Pen)Llwynrobert as well as the ancient farmstead at Cilonnen. The dense wet woods of the valley itself were still almost untouched. Such was the growth of the population at this end of the parish that the little chapel at Llanyrnewyr (to use an older spelling) became the customary chapel for that area in 1583 and, from then on, the parish was increasingly regarded as being in two parts - 'higher' and 'lower'. Part of the impetus for the development of this area was almost certainly the exploiting of coal. In Elizabethan times we have evidence that a road existed from Crofty, climbing through a string of settlements at Kingie, Cwm Cynnar, Rallt, Tir Lleyky and Cae Cenwyn on its way to Port Eynon. This was surely the first of the 'coal roads' by which the east end of the parish traded with the rest of the Gower peninsula.

In the western part of the parish most of the common land was left intact. The common land was a vital part of the agricultural economy for local farmers who pastured their cattle and sheep there. In Subboscus, however, it is likely that substantial areas of common and moor land were enclosed by local farmers as is apparent in the litigation conducted by the Earl of Worcester against the encroachers. It appears that Welshmoor was much encroached on from the direction of Cillibion and Llethrid Farms which were largely outside the manor of Landimore. Elsewhere, farms such as Crickton and Freedown edged the moorland and no advance has been made since.

The Valor Ecclesiasticus of 1535, the subsidy assessment roll of 1543 and a survey of the diocese of St David's in 1582 give us sufficient details to draw some conclusions about the size and nature of the population in the parish during the 16th century. Between 119 and 162 households were accounted for in the assessments. Various means of calculating the population may be used and these will provide figures of between 475 and about 900 for the parish. Because these assessments probably ignored a significant number of people, not eligible for tax on account of their poverty, the higher of these two figures is likely to be nearer the truth. We should assume, therefore, that the number of people living in Llanrhidian parish in the later Tudor period was between 700 and 900, and rising. The 1543 assessment also tells us that these people were largely of the poorest categories eligible for taxation. In this respect Llanrhidian was almost the poorest parish in the peninsula (neighbouring Cheriton was possibly worst-off) and only 2 of the inhabitants appear to have had yeoman farmer status. At a guess the farms at Cillibion, Leason, Wernhalog, Pencaerfenni and Killan were likely to have housed the 'wealthiest' of the farmers. On the whole, however, it is clear that the populace of Llanrhidian was poor by both Gower and Glamorgan standards. The concentration of capital and wealth in nearby Swansea, even at this early period, probably had a detrimental effect on the local economy.

The First Coal Mines

While Sir Rhys ap Thomas was adapting the castle at Weobley to be a fitting home for an ambitious Tudor courtier, the other end of the parish was seeing a very different kind of development. It is very probable that excavation of coal from 'crop holes' had gone on before 1500 but it is only in latter half of the sixteenth century, from around 1580, that we find evidence for the activity that was to dominate the economic life of the area for 400 years. The port books for south Wales reveal that during the period 1560 to 1603 there was a hundredfold increase in shipping in the Burry estuary. That such an increase could be accounted for in any other way than the export of coals is unthinkable. The Burry estuary, as a port, comprised the north and south sides of the river so we must allow that a significant part of this trade was from the Carmarthenshire coast.

Certainly, the trade in Llanrhidian parish was of a small scale by later standards. Most of the coal would have been sold at the pithead and the mines themselves were probably small 'bell-pits' for the most part. John Lucas, of the Stouthall estate near Reynoldston, bought a parcel of lands around Llanmorlais, probably stretching up onto the Wern and this was clearly for the purpose of coal extraction. Considerable capital would be needed for these operations, capital which was lacking in this poor parish. It is likely, therefore, that other early operations were financed by Swansea merchants. The proximity of good seams of coal outcropping so close to a navigable seaway would have made the prospect of investing in the Morlais valley mines an attractive one.

There is evidence, however, that one syndicate of local farmers was working coal mines just to the east of the Wern. David Robert Hopkin, farmer at Pencaerfenni and Crofty, wrote his will in 1596 and left to his wife, Margaret, his *'myne of coles and the proffite thereof'*. David died in 1599 and his estate passed to his son Evan. In the will of William ap William (d. 1609) we find that Evan was a partner in a mining operation together with a George David Morgan and William ap William himself. In 1609 there was coal to the value of £5 at the pit head and 2 pits open. When David Morgan died in 1624 the mines were still operating. David left to his son Robert *'the third pte of all the coal and pfittes of coals at lloyn Thomas'*. Llwyn Thomas is a field on the south side of the Morlais valley less than a mile from where the stream reaches the estuary. From the north side of the valley the field can still be seen today together with the hummocks left by these late Tudor mines. Very likely it was not, then, so much a field as a clearing in the dense oak woods that cloaked the valley sides.

Llwyn Thomas - looking west over Crofty. The uneven nature of the ground, which is due to the Tudor mine workings, is readily apparent.

The Morlais Valley at the end of the Tudor period.

C - site of mining operation

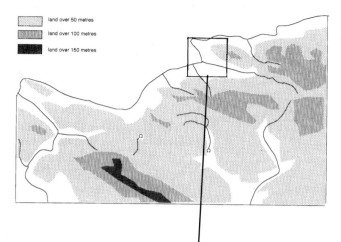

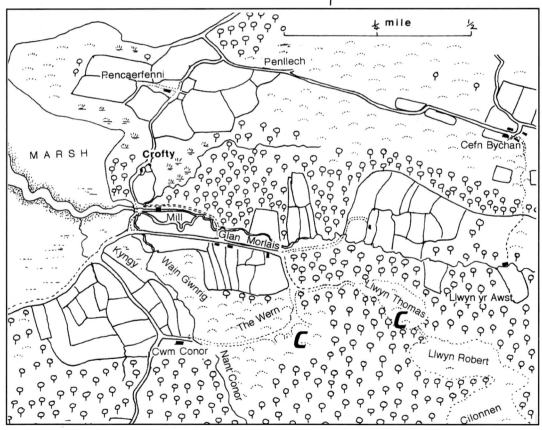

At this time the area was still characterised by scattered farms and, probably, large areas of woodland. Crofty and Llanmorlais would not have been recognised as villages.

Mills

As magnets for early settlement, mills almost equalled churches in importance. The old manor of Landimore was well served by the mills on the Burry stream of which there were, at one time, seven. One of these mills, the Stone Mill just upstream of Cheriton, was the custom mill for the manor which meant that tenants had to have their corn ground there upon penalty of a fine. This 'suit of mill' had significance for farmers right across Llanrhidian which was very largely a part of the manor of Landimore. Clearly some farmers preferred to pay the fine and use mills nearer home rather than make the arduous journey across the length of the parish with their corn. At one time or another there were at least seven mills in the parish and possibly an eighth at Leason. There were five watermills (three at Lanrhidian, one at Llanmorlais and one at Penclawdd) and two windmills (one near Weobley and the other at Cilonnen). With one exception these were all 'corn grist mills', the needs of the woollen industry were largely met by mills outside the parish.

The first reference to milling in the parish is in a grant of 1375 of the moiety (half share) of the Nether Mill at Llanrhidian to Meuric ap Philip. The name 'Nether Mill' (meaning 'lower mill') presupposes the existence of a higher mill and we thus conclude that by this date there were two mills in the village. A document of 1323 makes reference to two mills and a weir in Landimore and Llanrhidian, it may well refer to the village mills. In 1400 Richard Scurlage held a mill in the village and it was worth 40 shillings. By the mid-Tudor period it would appear that all four watermills in the parish were in operation. Unfortunately for us, it is difficult to trace the histories of the mills in great detail because, in wills and surveys, they are often referred to merely as *grist mills lying within the parish of Llanrhidian* and hence could be in any part of the parish. The following account is an attempt to untangle some of the threads of their various histories.

Llanrhidian Higher Mill.

This mill was of medieval origins. It stood by the church at a point where a spring still gushes out of the hillside. This spring has the virtue of being remarkably consistent in its flow. In 1632 the mill was held under the manor of Nicholaston by John William Griffith and Phillip Robert, it was described as *'one griste water mill at Llanridien called the Upper mill, and a little plot of ground thereunto adjoyninge...'* . Later, the mill was owned by John Williams (possibly the same John William Griffith) but on his death in 1655 it appears that the mill came into the hands of the Gwyn family. Anthony Gwyn, who died in 1663, left the mill to his four daughters until his son Richard should wish to buy it. He calculated that the annual value of the mill by that time was £26 and he wished this sum to be put towards his desire that *'my children be cept att skoole for to reead and .... some of the rent of the mille goes to pay for there lerninge....'*. Because the Upper Mill continued to be held outside the manor of Landimore it does not feature in its surveys and rent rolls. We do know that Richard took over the mill and that it

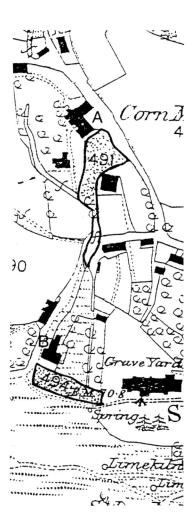

The two Llanrhidian mills as they are depicted on the 1878 map of the village. The Lower MIll is marked 'A', the Higher Mill is marked 'B'. The two millponds are stippled (nos. 491 and 494.)
Reproduced from the 1879 Ordnance Survey map.

31

remained in the Gwyn family into the 18th century. In 1844, at the time of the tithe assessment, the owner was Charles Gwynne (possibly a descendant of Anthony Gwynne) and the tenant Christopher Long Badcock, with his Somerset wife Ann Maria, a dressmaker. The mill fell into disuse when, in 1860, Badcock was gaoled for 4 years for stealing chicken from Leason. Today the site is being re-used but excavations have shown the extent of the mill pond and the little mill house set immediately below the pond.

Llanrhidian Lower Mill.

As shown above, the lower mill was in existence in the late medieval period. It owed its existence to the fact that the stream that issues at the site of the upper mill continues to flow steeply down to the marsh enabling a good head of water to be created by a second millpond. This enabled the last mill house erected on the site (and happily still standing) to accommodate the largest wheel in Gower. The only direct early reference this writer has found to the Lower Mill, apart from that of 1375, is that in the will of John Harry who died in 1668. He was the farmer of Tir Coch further up the parish but the chattel lease of the Lower Mill is mentioned in his inventory as worth £3 : 10s. . The reconstruction of this mill in 1803 is detailed by a plaque set in the wall stating that it was built *'at the sole expense of Wm. M. Evans, Gent'* . The masons were John Bynon and Evan Jenkin, the carpenters William Edward and George Evans. In 1844 the miller was William David whose widow was carrying on the work 17 years later. Today, the defunct mill still stands in good repair, one of the most endearing of Gower's buildings.

Llanrhidian Lower Mill.

Crofty Mill.

If the early 16th century reference to the four mills of Llanrhidian (Penrice and Margam mss. calender no. 3002) refers to the watermills of the parish then both Crofty and Penclawdd mills were in existence by that time. The earliest direct reference to the mill at Crofty is in 1625. The will of a local yeoman, Philip John Richard Hopkin, refers to his *'water grist mill called Morleys Mill'*. The will makes it clear that this mill was at Crofty and probably belonged to the former estate of David Robert Hopkin of Pencaerfenni and Crofty. The mill was held on a rent of £7. The details of the will are sometimes difficult to interpret, many of the field names have since been lost, but it seems likely that the mill was part of what became Gelli-on Farm to which it was adjacent. Although the Morlais stream is by far the biggest in the parish it is inclined to great variations in flow and sometimes dries to little more than a trickle. The mill, close to the point where the stream flows into the marsh, had no mill pond and was fed by a leat from the stream about 200 metres higher up, close to the present day garage at Llanmorlais Cross. There was very little fall in the stream over this distance and the mill wheel must have been 'undershot' (driven by water flowing under the wheel). All this suggests a small mill, capable of limited output and dependent on the flow of the stream on any one day. In 1770 the farmer at the adjacent farm of Gelli-on was Thomas Lloyd and it was his son, Thomas Lloyd (born

The Crofty Mill building as it appeared early in the twentieth century when it had long been in disuse.

1808), who was miller in the 1851 census. The mill closed in 1860, according to local lore, and Thomas, who died in 1883, lies buried outside the doorway of Llanrhidian Church.

Meyrick's Mill - Penclawdd.

The first direct reference to the mill at Penclawdd is in the will of Owen Matthew dated 1681. As we have noted earlier, it is probable that this mill is a great deal older than that. The mill always appears to have been known as 'Meirick's Mill', in the 19th century it was given the Welsh equivalent name of 'Melin Meurig'. It straddles the little Cedi stream flowing down from the high ground north of Three Crosses. Whilst not having a great flow of water this stream falls steeply in its lower reaches and a mill pond at the strategic point by Parc Hendy Farm created a good head of water. The pond was long and narrow, constricted by the valley in which it lay, and one suspects that it would not have sustained lengthy periods of milling in drier weather. There are 19th century records of a number of millers: David Gregory (c1841), David Jenkin (c1844) and Thomas William (c1881). The mill closed before that century was out but survives substantially in the form of the present day residence on the site.

Leason Mill. (O.S. ref. 483927)

This mill, identified by Bryan Taylor in his 1991 survey of Gower mills (Gower Magazine 42), is one of Gower's more enigmatic buildings. The site and building strongly suggest that this was a mill. It stands at the foot of the hill below Leason at a point where a strong stream of water springs from the hillside. It would have been the only watermill in that part of the manor of Weobley but there is no reference to any such mill in the surveys. The reference to Ezra Griffith's grist mill in the manor of Weobley in 1692 has been taken to refer to Leason mill but this is unlikely - it may refer to the Crofty mill (which lay within the manor) but most likely to the Derlwyn Mill in Bishopston which was also in the manor and owned, in 1665, by Henry Griffith. The mill is referred to directly, however, in the Llanrhidian Vestry Book in the 1830's. One suspects that it may have experienced desultory use during the 18th and early 19th centuries.

Windmills.

Almost nothing at all is known about Llanrhidian's windmills but that they existed. Cilonnen's windmill occupied a site about 100 metres south of the road between Cilonnen and Gelli Groes, the site is all grass now but would doubtless reveal some foundations. Rentals and surveys between 1755 and 1763 refer to the 'old windmill' at Cilonnen occupied by John Bowen of Cilonnen Fach. A manuscript dating c.1665 (Penrice and Margam no. 1670) relating to the Cilonnen and Llanmorlais area has a scribbled note on the back to remind the writer about a tenant for the windmill. It is highly likely that this refers to Cilonnen mill. It is shown to be standing on Yates's 1799 map of the area, described as 'Old Windmill'.

In the lower division the post-medieval Windmill Farm may have

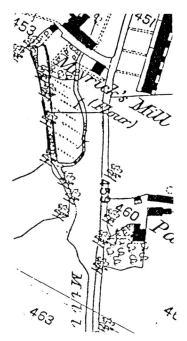

Meyrick's Mill as it appears on the 1878 Ordnance Survey map. The mill pond is long and narrow, to the top left of the map. Reproduced from the 1879 Ordnance Survey map.

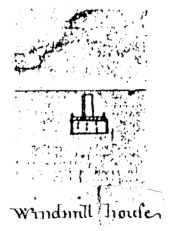

The depiction of Windmill Farm on the 1785 estate map held in the Swansea record office. Whether the 'Tower' is in fact a depiction of a yard at the back of the farm cannot be said.
Reproduced by kind permission of the County Archivist, West Glamorgan Archive Service. D/DP811

derived its name from having a windmill incorporated into its structure. This is suggested by the drawing of the farm in John William's estate map of 1785 but this drawing is ambiguous. There are no references to a windmill operating in this part of the parish.

Staffal Haegr.

The only woollen mill in the parish, this was established by the Dix family in the early 19th century and ran until 1904. The mill wheel was driven from a leat that intercepted the stream between Llanrhidian's Higher and Lower mills. The leat led across the fields for 400 metres and delivered water to the top of the wheel. The woollen factory was appended to, or adapted from, the old farm buildings which dated from at least Tudor times.

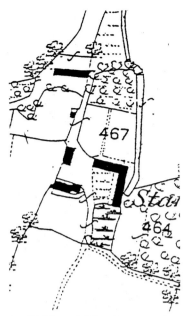

Staffal Haegr Mill as it appeared on the 1879 Ordnance Survey Map

Staffal Haegr mill today - the mill is the wing on the right of the picture with a pond, out of sight behind the foreground shrubs, immediately above it.

Testamentary Evidence

Emerging from the Tudor period we are suddenly confronted with a relative wealth of documentary evidence for the parish. There are surveys, rentals, manor court records, leases and deeds, but none more important for discovering the details of daily life than the wills made by parishioners. These give an unique insight into the homes of the wealthy, the farmers and the poorer people. Through their wills we hear, for the first time, the words and thoughts of the ordinary people who lived in Llanrhidian and discover what it was like to live in north Gower in the post-Tudor period. This chapter is based on a survey of 120 wills written between 1600 and 1700 and the general picture built up as a result can be taken to be indicative of the general conditions of life in the area. Most wills divide into two parts. In the first part the testator commended his or her life to God and then proceeded to disperse his estate to charity, relatives and friends, making special provisions where necessary. The second part of the will consists of an inventory of the testator's possessions made by neighbours soon after his death; this inventory establishes the value of the testator's estate for the purpose of the probate charge. It is this inventory that gives us such detailed information about the farms and households of the period.

Rich and Poor in Llanrhidian

The first impression gained from looking at these wills is of the poverty of the inhabitants. Glamorgan was not a wealthy area by British standards. Across the Bristol Channel, in Devon, standards of living appear to have been generally higher. But even compared with Glamorgan people, the homes of Llanrhidian were poor.

A survey of wills of the same period in West Glamorgan by Emery (in National Library of Wales Journal, *West Glamorgan Farming*) suggests that on a percentage basis there were more testators in the poorest category in Llanrhidian than in Glamorgan generally. Over 50% of the Llanrhidian testators had inventories valued below £20. At the other end of the social spectrum there were a few relatively wealthy households. Evan Seyes of Killan (d.1683) appears to have been a comfortably well-off ex-military man with an inventory valued at over £209. Even better-off was Henry Bowen of Llanelen (d1640), a farmer on a large scale. Such men would have been regarded as comfortably-off in Devon, in Gower they would have been men-of-standing.

The concentration of extremely poor households in Llanrhidian makes it inevitable that there was a large number of inhabitants who left no will at all. Richard Harry, who died in 1630, left goods to the value of only £2 13s 10d (£2.69) but there were undoubtedly many poorer still for whom the business of writing up a will was an irrelevance. Such men and women were the subject of charitable donations many of which were made through the wills of their wealthier peers. David Robert Hopkin (d.1600), for example, left £2 for the *'poor men's box'*. This was an exceptional act of charity from one

The will of Ann Jenkins, died 1647, showing the inventory which was always appended to the end of the will.
(By permission of the National Library of Wales).

of the wealthier farmers (his inventory was valued at £72.87) and much smaller donations were the order of the day. In 1601 John Whityard (probably of Wimblewood) left a shilling (£0.05) to the poor of Llanrhidian and in 1605 Richard Gosse left just 2d (less than 1p) for the parish poor. Altogether, 27% of the testators made provisions of some sort for the poor. These provisions took forms other than money, especially from about 1645 onwards when Thomas Rees of Freedown left a bushel each of wheat and barley, a stone of cheese and a half gallon of butter to the poor. Often, testators would be more specific as to the recipients of these donations. As people became more accustomed to the division of the parish they were increasingly inclined to nominate which division should receive their gifts. Philip John of Penclawdd (d. 1647) left 3 bushells of corn (half barley and half oats) to the poor of the upper division of the parish whilst Marie Lewis (d. 1686) left one and a half bushels of barley to the poor of the lower division. Most specific of all were men like George Lucas who, in 1647, left *'to those that carry my corps un to burial 2 bushels of barley and 2 of oats'*. Harry Jenkin (d. 1629) willed *'to ffoure of the poor people of the parish of Lanrhidian that is to Jane Harry, to Ellen Richard, to Elizabeth Evan and to Jone Morgan to each of them half a peck of barley'*. In accordance with the poor law acts, charity would normally be distributed by the overseers of the poor. One such was Anthony Gwynne (d1663) of the Higher Mill, Llanrhidian, who was clearly an approachable man. On his death he had lent more than half the value of his estate to various people throughout the upper division of the parish.

The most consistent gift in the first half of the century was not, however, to the poor but to the reparation of the cathedral church of St Davids; in each case 4d (2p) was donated. Occasionally, small amounts of money were also left to the local church at Llanrhidian.

Occupations

One of the most striking features of wills of this period is the extent to which everybody depended on agriculture. On average, nearly 70% of the value of inventories was in agricultural stock of some sort. Yeomen and husbandmen all had between 60% and 100% of their wealth in the farm but also there were mine owners like David Robert Hopkin of Crofty who had 82% of his wealth in agriculture, weavers like David William John Robert (d. 1619) with 87% and tanners like Philip Harry Jenkin with 80% in agriculture. There were exceptions like Evan Long, a poor weaver, who had no farm stock at all (his inventory was only worth £2.93) but on the other hand John Leyson, a shipwright who died in 1690 had 77% of his wealth tied up in oxen, cows, horses, sheep and corn. In general, however, it can be seen that those who had least of their wealth tied up in agriculture were the very poorest members of the community, possibly explained by their old age and inability to manage an agricultural regime. Some tradesmen, too, were understandably less dependent on farming. The only apparent exception was Evan Seyes (d.1683) of Killan who maintained a substantial arable farm but had far more wealth in gold and silver stacked in his coffers than set out in the farm.

In the House

The inventories dramatically reveal details of farmhouse interiors. Items that would fetch a fortune in today's antique market but have long since gone to firewood are preserved in these often intimate records. The most striking feature of those old households, to the modern eye, would have been the barrenness of the rooms, the paucity of the furniture. Few homes, especially in the first half of the century, had anything that would be recognised today as a table, whilst chairs were just as uncommon. Planks, boards and occasionally trestles made do in many homes while stools and forms had to serve for seating. Not one settle is mentioned during the 17th century and it is likely that Owen Russell's (d.1642) 'turned chair' was the talk of all his visitors because of its rarity. Russell's inventory is so typical of the period that it is worth quoting in detail especially since it, rather unusually for the area, lists items room by room. In the hall, which was the central living area of the little home, were to be found a table board and frame, the turned chair, a cupboard and a great chest. Apart from furniture there were 5 brass pans, 2 brass pots, 1 iron pot, 2 brandirons and 2 brass candlesticks, 13 pewter platters and other 'small implements'. The only other room in the house, 'the chamber', contained the bed, more coffers, a sideboard and yet more 'small implements'. These items altogether were valued at just £4.75.

As the century wore on, tables became more commonplace. Thomas William (d1661) of Killan even had a round table whilst Katherine Bowen (d1698) had 2 little side tables. Coffers and chests were vital pieces of furniture if only for keeping vermin away from items like corn or linen. Evan Seyes of Killan, already mentioned, kept £27 worth of gold and nearly £32 of money in his coffer. Virtually every house had at least one coffer. There were also hutches and presses; the distinctions between such items were probably rather too subtle for us to guess but they were all lidded, usually locked, freestanding chests. Cupboards became increasingly common towards 1700.

The other principle item of furniture in the house was, of course, the bed. The more well-to-do generally had a feather bed valued at about £1 or more. Dust beds were, in all households, valued at about a quarter of the value of a feather bed. The mattresses were stuffed with chaff, woollen dust or whatever would serve. These were the beds of the poor and the servants. In the inventories, beds are usually mentioned 'with their appurtenances' and these are occasionally detailed as blankets, boulsters, coverlets and sheets. Soft furnishings were not typical of the homes but Henry Bowen, the wealthy farmer of Llanelen, had curtains, cushions and carpets. Carpets were very rare but the odd rug does appear. Clearly most people had a cold stone floor with, perhaps, a little straw spread over.

Clothes are rarely itemised. Edith Whityer of Wimblewood (d. 1623) left a smock, 2 breeches, petticoats and 2 waistcoats. David Harry of Penrallt (d.1635) left his best cloak, doublet and hose. Jerkins and stockings are also mentioned.

Cast-iron cooking pots such as this were the mainstay of culinary equipment.

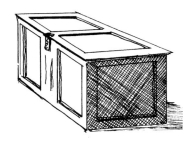

Coffers were vital for keeping valuables and important household goods.

A Skillet

A Cauldron

Around the house were also other prized items. Candlesticks, often of brass and occasionally pewter, were common and a useful advance on crude rush lights. David Harry and Harry Owen both had clocks which probably made them useful to neighbours. John Richard Dunne (d. 1614) may have been proud of his salt cellar since few others appear to have owned such a luxury. Henry Bowen of Llanelen had a Bible and other books, quite exceptional in 100 years of inventories in Llanrhidian. A little more common were weapons; Evan Seyes of Killan still had his sword which may have been used in the Civil War. Henry Bowen (Llanelen) was clearly an ex-soldier with '1 muskett and the furniture for a little horse and other armes for warre' together with a 'flagge in a silver cover'. Griffith John Nicholas (d. 1631) also left ' 1 mysked with his appurtenances and a sword'. Less warlike was the fowling piece left by John Walter (d. 1667).

For the fireplace we find detailed accounts of the pots and pans used. The basic kitchen would have 2 or 3 crocks and some brass pans. Frying pans, skillets, cauldrons and posnets (long handled cooking pots) were also to be found. Maud Thomas (d. 1616) left a furne (a baking pot) but presumably most baking was done in the bread oven set in the wall. The bakestone was by no means uncommon whilst spits and andirons were additional means of cooking by roasting in front of the open fire. Brandirons were large trivets supporting cooking vessels above the fire, alternatively pot hooks enabled crocks and cauldrons to be suspended over the flames at varying heights.

Food was served on platters. Those made of wood, 'trenchers', were possibly beneath being mentioned but pewter platters were certainly worth having a valuation put on them. They were worth more than a shilling each (£0.05) so Harry John Leyson's (d. 1641) 25 platters and 4 dishes of pewter required mentioning. Cups, spoons, salt cellars, saucers and flagons were all to be found fashioned in pewter and among the prided objects of the household.

More ambitious cooking operations required larger vessels, brewing pans, vats, barrels and 'timbring' vessels. 'Standards' would measure precise quantites such as pints and half pints. Some vessels strongly suggest the activity of the household - Nicholas Prichard of Penrallt (d. 1697) had a vat and an ale cask whilst Richard Clement the shoemaker (d. 1630) left a brewing vat, cooling vessels, a brewing cauldron and malt together with numerous other vats and cauldrons. The shipwright John Leyshon (d. 1690) had 3 brewing vats. Leyshon also had a churning vat - butter making was clearly a common occupation of the farmsteads. Matthew Richard (d. 1683) left a pot of butter when he died and Thomas Rees of Freedown (d. 1645) left half a gallon of butter to the poor. Butter is found in other households together with sides of bacon (Jenkin Long d. 1638) and joints of pork and beef. Jenkin Richard (d. 1621) left 2 flitches of bacon and 6d worth of pigs mourt (lard); he was a weaver by trade and also left 14 pounds of wool and a pair of looms.

Most tradesmen inevitably left some mark of their business. Tanners had hides tanning and training racks on which to stretch them. Both Harry Jenkin (d. 1629) and his son Philip Harry Jenkin (d. 1646) left hides and racks.

On the Farm

As we have seen, the farmers of Llanrhidian ranged from the desperately poor to the relatively wealthy. The average yeoman farmer left an inventory worth some £30 of which about three quarters in value was in agricultural stock. Typical of such farmers was Nicholas Prichard of Penrallt. The Prichards had farmed for a long time at Penrallt (between Llanrhidian and Leason) and continued to do so well into the 18th century. Nicholas, who died in 1697, was one of the less wealthy of the line. An examination of his agricultural stock will give a fair idea of what was to be found on the average farm of the lower division of the parish. The inventory lists this as :

> *1 yoke of oxen*
> *2 steers*
> *4 cows*
> *3 heifers and another steer*
> *1 mare and colt*
> *2 old horses*
> *20 store sheep*
> *15 ewes and 10 lambs*
> *hogs*
> *a moiety of a rick of wheat*
> *barley winnowed and unwinnowed*
> *half a bushel of oats*
> *implements of husbandry*

It is worth looking at each item in turn to understand the local farming economy. First of all, in most inventories, are the oxen, the tractors of the old farmyards. They were found on most farms except those of the very poorest. Some farmers had only one ox, it was exceeedingly rare for a farmer to have more than six. Wealthy Henry Bowen of Llanelen had 18 but his wealth probably represented the combined stock of Llanelen, Wernhalog and other nearby holdings. Oxen were good for tough land and, when too old to work, they could be sold for meat. But they were slow and needed good grass to replenish their strength. Some farms had working horses and these could be mixed with the oxen in harness, the horses leading the team. Horses were economical because they could be tethered on the marsh or common and could work the plough a little quicker. Also, the horses in the wills of the north Gower farmers were half the price of oxen which could cost up to £2 a head. During the 17th century horses were increasingly in demand for the local mines, particularly in carrying coals down to the estuary for shipment. So a farmer-cum-mine-owner (see 'A New Era') like David Robert Hopkin of Pencaerfenni had a ready use for his 17 horses.

Dairy cattle or 'kine' feature most significantly in all the farms of the period. Cows were an excellent investment for a small farmer like Nicholas Prichard because, even if their produce was not readily marketable, the milk, butter and cheese were useful in maintaining the family diet. Most farms had at least 3 cows, herds might be as large as 20 or more in some cases. Together with the heifers, calves

Oxen were the mainstay of many farms until well into the 19th century. The author has heard local people speak of their forebears singing to the oxen as they ploughed and moving them on by pricking their heels with a pointed stick.

and store cattle (bullocks and steers) they usually accounted for more than half of the value of the agricultural stock on most farms. With an abundance of well watered meadows and very extensive pastures, cattle were clearly a sensible and economic choice for the farmer. The cows were clearly the local red cows of Glamorgan; there are references to red heifers and cows. Griffith John Nicholas (d. 1631), for example, left 2 'red heyfers', one of them to Margaret Thomas. Like the Devon cattle, they were small and 'pretty' animals. There are also some references to the black cattle which were native to Gower. Local cheese, reputedly something between a Gloucester and a Cheshire in type, was of high quality and the butter was also highly regarded. Apart from the dairy products there was also meat and leather from the herds, or else the animals could be sold in Swansea. Animal prices across the Bristol Channel in Devon were consistently much higher than in Gower and there was a steady trade in cattle being shipped from Port Eynon and Oxwich. The road from Llanmorlais to Port Eynon was clearly established by this time and we can guess that both cattle and coal made up much of its traffic.

Sheep featured strongly on many farms, especially in the western half of the parish. Nicholas Prichard's 45 sheep were typical of that part of Llanrhidian. 50 years before, when old Robert Prichard was running the farm, Penrallt had some 200 sheep. Since then prices had declined and farms had looked to mix their economies more. Within a year of Nicholas's death the farm had moved strongly towards arable but 20 years later the flocks were back up to full strength. The native breed was the Glamorgan Down sheep, small but of high quality. Producing fine wool, it could support the local weavers and feature amongst the exports to Devon.

Apart from these mainstays, there were other kinds of livestock. Most farms and households had one or two pigs (useful for bacon), together with geese and chicken. Even today it is not unusual to see a gaggle of geese on the marsh, 300 years ago it must have been a common sight. A little less common around the parish were goats. Jenkin John (d. 1651) who lived in the upper division of the parish had '19 goats great and small', valued at £1. Honey was clearly part of the local economy. John Whityard (d. 1601), probably of Wimblewood, had '4 hives or stocks of bees', an item by no means unique in the inventories of Llanrhidian.

It is apparent that the importance of the arable aspects of farming could be measured through the number of oxen kept on the farm. Some of the poorer farmers, however, had to rely on hiring these animals to plough their fields. Nicholas Prichard, like most of the farmers, grew wheat, barley and oats. It is interesting that his wheat was in a 'moiety' of a rick. This sharing of the produce of a field surely indicates that some collaborative farming was still taking place at the end of the 17th century. Arable farming was more extensive on the limestone plateau in the lower division of the parish. John Donne (d. 1613), probably of Leason, had 3 acres of wheat, 4 acres of barley and 5 acres of oats. Thomas Rees (d. 1645) of Freedown had 2 acres of wheat, 5 acres of barley, 1 acre of oats and another acre of 'pease'. Oats featured a little more strongly in the upper division but it can be seen

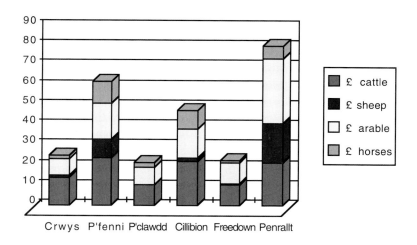

Early 17th century wills from Crwys, Pencaerfenni, Penclawdd, Cillibion, Freedown and Penrallt Farms, showing the value of each will in the principle areas of cattle, sheep, arable and horses.

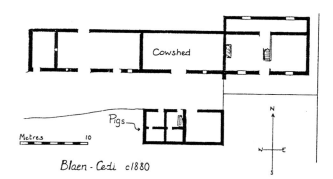

Blaen - Cedi c1880

Blaencedi Farm - developed in the area above Penclawdd near Blue Anchor - probably around 1700. A hundred years earlier its fields were common land and hedgerow surveys confirm a date of 1600 for enclosure. Originally a mixed farm, its fields are all now for grazing.

that barley was possibly the most widely grown crop. Barley bread was still the mainstay of these 17th century folk and baked right up to the beginning of this century. Barley, of course, had an additional use in brewing and, as we have seen, versatility was an important virtue to the farmer. References to other crops are rare, beans and peas are mentioned occasionally. When Henry Lucas bought some land on the Wern for coal mining he found that the local farmer had fenced the land for 'turneeps'.

Hay was an important crop and hayricks are occasionally mentioned. Mention is more often made of the 'haggard', a dialect word for the hay garth (the enclosure set aside for hayricks). Crofty still has its 'Haggard Cottage' next to Pencaerfenni Farm. The cottage stands inside the site of the actual haygarth. Dung was also held to be worth valueing though rarely at more than a few pence.

Haggard Cottage, Crofty, today. Originally the site of the 'hay guard' - where hay stacks for Pencaerfenni Farm (behind) stood.

Llanrhidian at Court

What mattered to the people of Llanrhidian in the 17th and 18th centuries was whether they could carry on their livelihood with little or no hindrance above what they owed to the local authority. For local people, that authority was chiefly the lord of the manor and it was his duty to see that people could carry on their livelihood in a reasonable way. The means by which this was done was the manor court. These courts, held every 6 months, enabled the lord to collect rents due to him, to see that proper means of maintaining order were maintained and to allow local people to bring petty grievances and nuisances to notice. Unfortunately for us, few of the court records survive and those which do, relating to the period between 1680 and 1750, reflect a period in which the influence of the courts was declining in the lives of ordinary people. Although the courts continued to be held until the early part of the 20th century they were, by that time, little more than a quaint archaism.

The bulk of the parish, lower and higher, was covered by the manors of Landimore and Weobley. Apart from the area immediately around Weobley Castle, the manor of Weobley also held land around Pencaerfenni Farm, Crofty and the western fringes of Penclawdd. The manor of Landimore extended well into the higher division of the parish as far as the banks of the Morlais stream and Penllwynrobert Farm. Most of the rest of the higher division of Llanrhidian belonged to the manor of Subboscus which answered to authorities in Swansea. One tiny slice, which was purchased by the Dunraven estate, in the middle of Penclawdd belonged to the manor of Henllys. 'Dunraven Close' commemorates this obscure connection in its name. Some individual holdings, such as the Higher Mill at Llanrhidian, also belonged to other manors.

Landimore and Weobley courts were held at both Llanrhidian and Reynoldston but increasingly at the latter which was more convenient to Penrice where the lord of the manor lived. The Subboscus courts were held in Swansea, most probably in the medieval 'Cross Keys' inn.

The proceedings of these courts reveal that enormous advantages of patronage lay with the lord of the manor or his representative. He could sanction fishing rights or permit coal to be laid down for shipping. He could insist that tenants grind their corn in his mill. At the time when these courts were recorded 'heriots' were still being paid. These were payments made on the death of a tenant by the heir to his or her estate. This payment of the best animal of the farm could be commuted to a money payment.

The following annotated transcript gives the flavour of these occasions. It is a record of a court held at Llanrhidian in September 1690. Proceedings at this court were rather brief, on some occasions there might be twice as many 'presentments' - if these were contentious, it is likely that the court sitting could take all day. When held in Reynoldston the court was in the local ale house which, presumably, made the day's sitting more enjoyable.

The Cross Keys Inn, Mary Street, Swansea, where Subboscus Courts were held in late medieval times.

*A presentiment made by the grand jury of the Mannor of Landimore att a **court Leet and Court Barron** held the 25th day of September 1690 att the dwelling house of Margarett Taylor before Thomas Mansell and George Thomas gent ther stewards.*

*Wee doe present all such as have made default of **suite of court** whome wee referre to the suite roule.*

Wee doe present Samuell Taylor to be resiant in the mannor of Landimore

Wee doe present John Price for leaveing his barne to be out of repair being prsented and to be repaired by John Price by next court

*Wee doe prsent David Bevan David Jenkin Harry Rowland to forme the office of **petty constables** in the lower division of the pish of Lanridian for the ensuing yeare.*

*Wee doe psent William Rogers and David Mayo to form the office of petty constable for **Rosilly** for this ensuing yeare*

Wee doe prsent John Tucker Robert Harry Philip Taylor Nicholas Horrod to form the office of petty constable in the pish of Cheriton for this ensuing yeare

*Wee doe psent the highway leading from Gowers Loade to the Marsh being the Kings Highway to be out of repaire and to be repaired by the higher division of the pish of Lanridian & yt hedges from **Lletty Lleyky** to the marsh to be shred by the owners thereof.*

*Wee doe psent David Jenkin for **leaving his piggs to be unringed** to the anoyance of the inhabytants thereabouts*

Wee doe psent George Rosser resiant within the said Lordshipp

We doe psent Richard Bydder for Hunting and killing hares within the Lordship of Landimore and pish of Rossilly without leave and licence of the Lord of the said Mannor

*Wee doe prsent John Tucker & Mathew Bennett for their **piggs to be unringd** to the anoyance of the inhabitance of the Lordshipp*

'Court leet...Court Barron' - The courts leet maintained the customs of the manor whilst the courts baron dealt with petty offences. In practice the two courts were held together.

'Suite of Court' - Tenants were obliged to be present at the courts and were liable to a fine if absent.

'Petty Constables' - extremely important to the general running of the community in terms of welfare as well as law and order, these appointments placed onerous duties on the recipients and were not always welcomed.

'Rhossili'- it must be remembered that Rhossili was still an important part of the manor of Landimore.

'Lletty Lleyky' - near the hamlet of the Rallt at the top of the hill above Llanforlais School

'Pigs .... unringed' - could be a serious nuisance in grubbing up commonly owned land.

The following entries are typical of proceedings during 1680 to 1740.

¶ *We doe ... prsent one white ram ye near yeare lop cut, and an half penny uppon, and under ye further eare a s....... One white whether ye neare eare forked & a halfpenny upon ye eare. And one white sheep ye neare yeare half penny upon and a square penny under ye further eare lop cutt, taken as estrayes in ye said Lordshipp.*

(Landimore Manor 1687. The sheep had various marks quaintly labelled and would have been kept in the pound. There were pounds at Three Crosses, Weobley and Landimore)

¶ *We doe ... likewise present David Jones of Gowers Load and John Lucas of Stouthall for breach of suit of mill in not grinding ye corne they use on ye Lords land ... at ye accustomed mill for ye said Lordship.* (Landimore court, 1687. Tenants were required to use the Lord's mill as stated, Jones and Lucas had probably used local mills and may have been prepared to pay the fine for the extra convenience.)

¶ *George William broke the common pound at Three Crosses to bring out his mare, put in the common fold by John Hinton for trespass* (Subboscus court 1691)

¶ *We doe present Sarah Marodeth for throwing of dunge into Evan Richard's gripe at Lanmorlais to the annoyance of Evan Richard being my lord's tenant.* (Landimore court 1713. A 'gripe' was a ditch, probably used for drainage.)

¶ *We psent Philip Jenkinson for repairing his stable at Polthybrage* (Landimore court 1713. Jenkinson, of Pwllybrag, was constantly in trouble for leaving his hedges and buildings in poor repair)

¶ *We doe present Mary David widdow of Pengarvenny for suffering her hedges to be out of repair between the lands of Calebb Thomas and the Common called the marsh att Crofte; she being a disturber (?) of impounding cattle upon her own neglect ....* (Weobley court, 1716. Mary's husband died 5 years previously and she was clearly in difficulty maintaining the farm.)

¶ *The jury doe meet at Leaston to set out a way to a field called Western Close at Leaston Wall.*(Weobley court, 1718. As the old open fields were enclosed tenants needed to maintain access to the fields still in common ownership.)

¶ *We do present John William for leaving a coal pitt open and useles on forrodi (Fairwood?) moor to the annoyance and danger of the highway.* (Weobley court, 1725)

¶ *We doe prsent George Gwyn for keeping a mangy horse being on the commons or highway* (Weobley court 1725)

¶ *We doe present Solomon Howell for building of a forge, an encroachment on the highway from Oldwalls to Lanridian.* (Weobley court 1727, The forge was opposite what is now Ebenezer Chapel and survives in part.)

¶ *A sufficient pair of stocks and a whipping post ought to be erected in Penclawdd .....at the expense of the inhabitants.* (Subboscus 1733)

The following text comes from a survey of the manor of Weobley made in 1665. These surveys, made on an almost annual basis, recorded the boundaries of the manor, its customs and the names of the freeholders and tenants within the bounds.

'There belongeth two court leets to bee held yearly for the said mannor to be houlden wthin the week next after May daie and wthin the week next after Michelmas day to wch Court all tenants freehoulders ....leashoulders ..... every tenant making default of doeing his suit is to be amerced six pence.

There is to Court barons to bee held for and wthin the sd mannor every three weeks as there is occasion........

The ffreehoulders in Soccage deyinge wth(in) ye said mannor payeth to the lord a heriott of the best liveing beast, and if a ffreehoulder daey out of the said mannor then there is due but five shillings ....

The royalties of waifes and strayes deodans fellons goods and forfeitures, tresure trove wreks when any happen are due to the lord of this mnaor.

And if a stranger die wthin the mannor the Lord shall hav his best beast, jewell or garment or other goods for a heriott..........

The royalties of hawking, hunting fishing and fowling belongeth to the lord of this mannor'

The ancient pound at Three Crosses actually survives and is part of the public house - 'The Poundfold'. The pound is the circular structure nearest the camera and has had a roof placed over it .

Walterston and Cillibion

Away on the southern edge of the parish, arguably on the least hospitable terrain within its boundaries, lies the remote settlement of Walterstone. A glance at the map shows that Walterstone is closer to Penmaen and Nicholaston than to Llanrhidian. As early as the medieval period, however, Walterstone was regarded as part of Llanrhidian's parish and so it is to this day. The origins of the settlement are not known but the name is highly suggestive of an Anglo-Norman farm created at the time of their first incursions into the area around 1100; the name means 'Walter's farm'. Together with other outlying hamlets such as at Cefn Bychan and Llanelen it appears that Walterstone had its own chapel which was subsidiary to the main church at Llanrhidian. This chapel was granted, with the church at Llanrhidian, to the Knights of St John during the 12th century but the land of what became known as 'the manor of Walterstone' was granted to the Cistercian monastery of Neath during the following century. The subsequent history of the ownership of the manor has been described fully by David Rees (Walterston: an old Gower settlement. *Gower 35*). In summary, it was held by the Cistercians until the Dissolution of monastic properties in 1536 after which it was sold, eventually, to the wealthy Price family of Cwrt-y-Carnau. Later, in the early 18th century, the manor passed to the Mansel estate and subsequently belonged to the Penrice and Margam estate until this century.

The original settlement, probably consisting of little more than a farm with one or two outlying houses for labourers, may have centred on what is now known as 'Little Walterstone'. Were it not for the recent identification of a 'lost village' site just to the west of 'Great Walterston', the whole area might not deserve more than passing interest as a parcel of farmlands and scattered farmsteads dating from the late medieval period. This site (at O.S. reference 508897) is believed to exhibit remains of up to 6 cottages with their 'tofts' or garden areas. It lies at the south west end of a parcel of lands known as the 'Sleng' whose tithes belonged not to the church but to the lord of the manor. Various sites have been proposed for the lost 'villa Walteri' apart from the abandoned settlement mentioned above but these are highly conjectural and lack supporting evidence. It is highly unlikely that such poor land could have supported more than a very small community which has been in decline since at least 1689 (the time of the earliest survey in our possession) and probably from the time of the Black Death. Even in 1689 the population seemed insufficient to occupy all the probable sites of homes and farms. The field boundaries on the map strongly suggest that enclosure of the Walterstone lands took place in phases extending the fields northwards from the 'Sleng' which was probably the original grange farm of the Cistercians. In the course of this enclosure of what must have been moorland much like the rest of Cefn Bryn's northward slopes, some older features were overlain. Among these was the lane leading from Cefn Bryn through the 'wood of Bruiz' to the 'vill of Penmaen', a track which at one time marked the northward extent of enclosure. The significance of this trackway has

The site of the lost village of Walterston still exhibits recognisable remains.

Great Walterston

been examined in detail by L A Toft in the 'Gower' magazine (no. 40). It strongly suggests that the ancient hunting park of the de Breos family, to which the manorial lands of Walterstone adjoin, dates from the early 13th century. The hedge boundaries indicate that the bulk of the enclosure of the Walterstone lands took place after the creation of Parc le Breos between 1220 and 1232.

Another feature overlain by the extending fields of the Walterstone settlement is an old lane (marked A - B on the map opposite) travelling directly northwards towards the old Welsh settlement of Cillibion. This ancient hamlet bordering the northern limits of the moors of Cefn Bryn probably predates Walterstone. During the early years of the existence of the latter it is likely that they viewed each other across a mile of empty moor and waste but were connected by this track. The Cillibion fields were probably centred on what is now called 'Little Cillibion' and, being part of a Welsh settlement, remained like that until Tudor times because the Welsh had lost the power to make territorial expansions of even the most limited nature. Meanwhile, the inhabitants of Cillibion could watch the steady expansion of Walterstone's fields enclosing the moors along the western edge of Parc le Breos. The later expansion of Cillibion and neighbouring farms is evidenced by the fields bordering Welsh Moor, the northern limit before that area reverted to woodland as a plantation in the 19th century. These fields were, in part, known as 'Queen's Meadows' in the mid 17th century; the name suggests that they were enclosed during the reign of Elizabeth I.

The detailed survey of the 'Manor of Walterstone and Kellylybion' made in 1689 gives us an interesting snapshot of the local economy. Whilst the details of tithe collection were of importance to the landowners and farmers of the 'Sleng' (the tithes there belonged to the lord of the manor) the right to collect furze and fern was probably of more importance to the lesser inhabitants of Walterstone and Cillibion. This important resource, gathered from Monkton Wood (at the eastern end of the Sleng) and Broadmoor (between Broad Pool and Cillibion) could be used for animal feed and bedding. Another use of furze was for heating the old ovens, in the words of the old Dorset poet William Barnes

'An then, when I ha' nothen else to do
Why I can teake my hook an' gloves an go
To cut a lot o' vuzz and briars
Vor heten ovens, or lighten viers.'

A number of references in the survey show that there was active encroachment on the moorland by peasant farmers. For example, it was noted that 'one Evan Bynon did .... erecte & encroach a house, & outhouses, & a garden, & a little croft upon the highway or wast land contiguously adjoineing the freehould lands late of George Lucas gentleman'. If Evan Bynon could have established his right to pasture cattle on the common as the other tenants did then he could manage to subsist with a very small enclosed holding. The wealthier farmers in the Sleng may have benefitted from a more mixed farming economy if the indication of their tithes - corn, grain, hay, hemp, flax, hops, honey, apples and eggs - is not just a catch-all formula. The inventories of parish wills suggest that all such produce was to be found in the area.

Walterston Cross or Corner - one of a number of abandoned homes on the fringes of the Walterston lands.

In the latter part of the 19th century a large portion of the enclosed land between Cillibion and Walterstone was converted to use as a duck shooting area centred on a decoy pond.

The 'manors' of Walterston and Cillibion c1900. 'The Sleng' is the shaded area at the south end of the estate. Points A and B appear to align with an old trackway - a line with which the boundary of Parc le Breos also aligned in the 13th century.

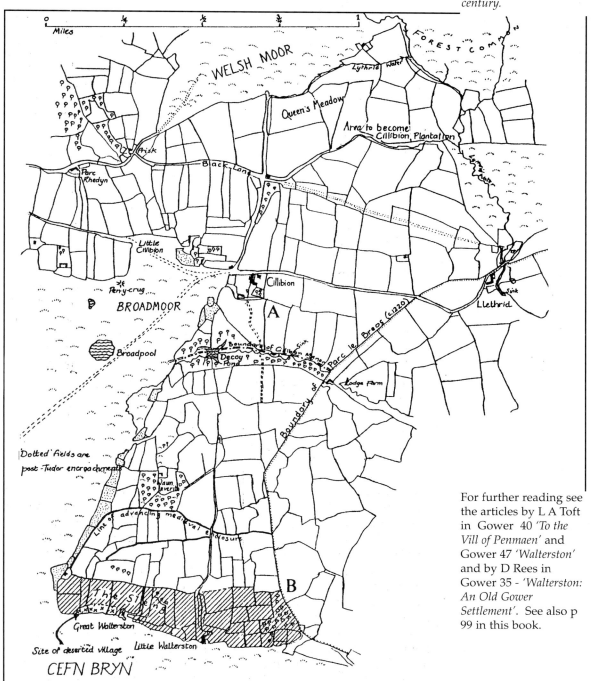

For further reading see the articles by L A Toft in Gower 40 'To the Vill of Penmaen' and Gower 47 'Walterston' and by D Rees in Gower 35 - 'Walterston: An Old Gower Settlement'. See also p 99 in this book.

Llanrhidian - the Village

There is evidence for a settlement at Llanrhidian in very early times and this settlement may have been connected with the great hillfort on nearby Cil-Ifor Top. The Leper Stone in Llanrhidian Church dating from pre-Norman times, the likelihood of an early Celtic foundation (possibly 6th century) for the church itself and the presence, by about 1300, of the infrastructure of a fully working agricultural community all point to the early historic origins of this village. Why should a settlement grow just at this point? The two excellent springs at the foot of the steep escarpment must have been a major attraction of the site and the church was founded between these springs (although relatively much closer to the higher spring which feeds the mill stream). Right across Europe, it was typical for villages to be established at points where different types of land use or potential were adjacent so that inhabitants had equal access to both. In Llanrhidian we have not only the boundary between the lower marshlands of the estuary and the higher plateau lands of Gower but also a boundary between the limestone lands of the west and the more acid woodlands and pastures to the east. With two good springs and some excellent potential for making level and fertile enclosures, Llanrhidian must have appeared to be one of Gower's most promising sites.

Since both mills appear to have been operating by 1375 it is reasonable to assume that, by the late medieval period, Llanrhidian was a well developed agricultural community. Clues as to what the village was like at this time are hard to find and to some extent we are forced to rely on the evidence of the relics of the medieval infrastructure that can be discerned either today or in the earliest maps of the village. An estate map of 1785 and the tithe map of c1840 reveal that elements of the medieval field system and of its ownership pattern had survived into the 19th century. Some 6 or 7 villagers had ownership of strips within fields close by the village and also at a little distance. These same villagers had ownership of a group of cottages or farms close by the church, exactly where the old village centre might have been expected. It is possible, thus, to make a tentative reconstruction of the medieval village - a cluster of small farms, a church, 2 mills, 2 springs and lanes leading to the marsh, to the common fields or to neighbouring communities. The earliest surviving survey of Llanrhidian dating from 1598 supports this picture. Within the village at that time there appear to have been not more than 7 freeholders - probably commensurate with the number of farms in the community. A manuscript of 1700 (Penrice and Margam 3604) refers, in a telling phrase, to mortgages for the 'upper and lower farms' at Llanrhidian. This appears to be a reference to the farming of what used to be a common field south of the highway leading from Swansea to Llangennith that was, by then, worked by the farmers of the village on a private basis. Farms such as Penrallt would qualify to be known as the 'upper farm' by virtue of working what was, originally, the higher common field. The village fields also extended towards the marsh - as early as 1400 there is a reference to '2 acres of land and salt meadow at Llanrhidian' and enclosure took place steadily from then on.

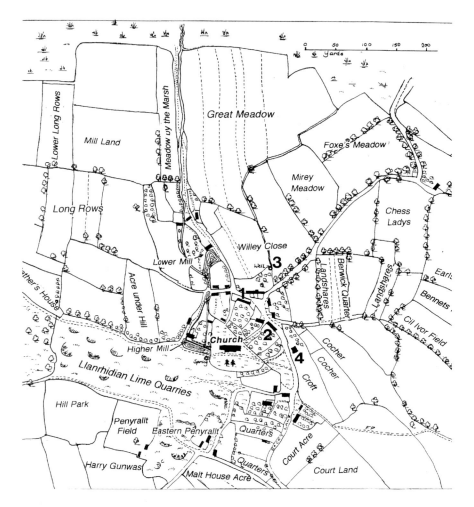

In 1851 the population of the village 'cluster' was 111. Using evidence from maps and surveys one can make a tentative estimate that in 1795 the population might have been nearer 90-100 and that in 1600 possibly not more than 60 or 70 persons. Nearly all those people would have been engaged in the farming of the fields around the village and a great deal of that farming was on a communal basis. Not all the villagers, however, depended directly on the land although their wills reveal that they all owned livestock or farm goods. An early record of 1676 mentions Howell David, a chair-maker, whilst in 1744 George David practised his trade of weaver in the village. David had a garden and possibly his cottage adjoining the churchyard. His probable forebear, Thomas David of Llanrhidian, was also a weaver when he gained a lease of Weobley Castle from William Seys in 1638. In 1595 David Geffrey, a 'shoemaker of Llanrhidian', was granted land at Cilivor by his father. At an even earlier period it is clear that the village had at least two millers, not a small number for any community. By the mid 19th century the census returns reveal that Llanrhidian could boast 2 millers, 4 dressmakers, 3 shopkeepers, a bookseller, 2 teachers, 2 carpenters, 3 tailors, a cordwainer (shoemaker), a cooper, 2 innkeepers or victuallers and 3 handloom weavers. In addition, there were agricultural labourers, a couple of colliers and even a horsebreaker. The arrival of the Post Office, in 1890, added yet further to the range of services then available in the village. Nearby Staval Hagar was also a scene of lively activity with George Dix's woollen factory employing at least another 6 weavers (see 'Llanrhidian's Woollen Industry').

Llanrhidian, at some time, was evidently a busy quarrying village. There is no record of this activity but a manor record of 1665 notes

> *The pcell of comon called Lanrhidians hill, and Alt comon are also ye lord's comons the tenants houlding of the lord of this mannor having libertie to dig stones for building and to make lyme for improving their lands, and also to have comon of pasture wth their cattle (Penrice and Margam no 1675-7).*

Limestone quarrying was active in north Gower from late Tudor times until the beginning of this century and Llanrhidian's quarries were, presumably operating over some of that period.

Opposite - the village c1840

1 - the original site of the school
2 - the schoolmaster's house (still standing)
3 - 'Rocky lane'
4 - Tir y Marchant, the centre of the old village
5 - Eastern Pen yr Allt Farm
6 - the Llanrhidian limestone quarries
7 - Llanrhidian Church
8 - Llanrhidian Upper Mill, where the the miller, Christopher Long Batcock, was convicted of sheep stealing from the marsh
9 - he Lower Mill, rebuilt in 1803
10 - the Welcome to Town Inn
11 - the Dolphin Inn
12 - the well which is reputed to have flowed with milk in 1185

Llanrhidian village depicted on a map of 1798 . The accompanying text reads - 'Llanrhidian Fairs are always kept on the Waste above the Cross which belong (sic) to Tir y Merchant. The Tenants there have always to thid Day raised the Tolls from all Standings and Booths which are Erected there at the Fair time - the Sawpitt belongs to this Tenement'
Reproduced by kind permission of the County Archivist, West Glamorgan Archive Service.
D/D BF E/1

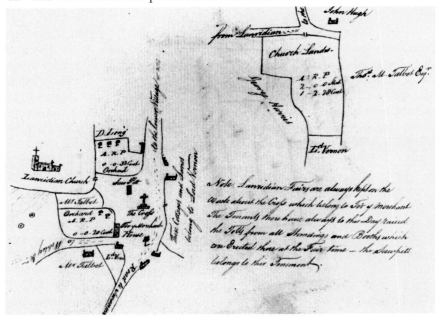

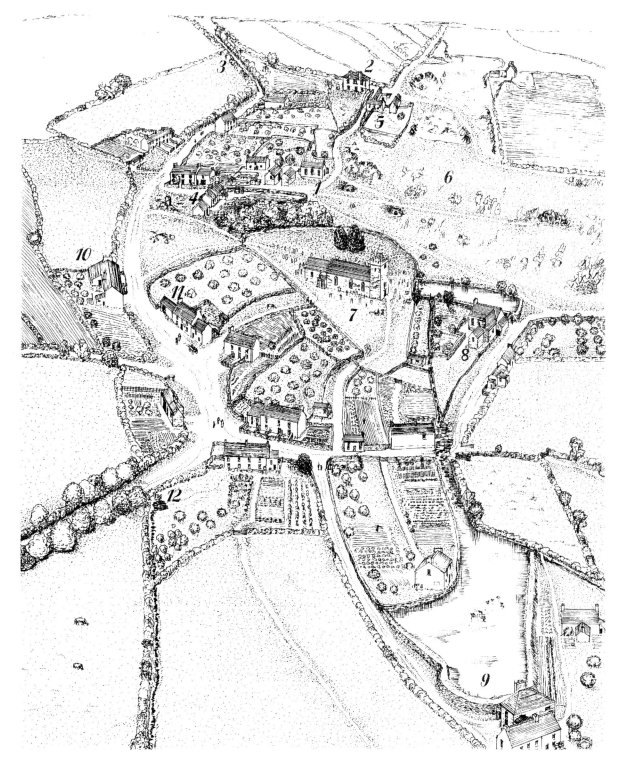

This is a reconstruction of the village around 1850. At that time, both mills were working and the village was predominantly a farming community. The view is looking south from the marsh end of the village. The lane disappearing off the bottom right hand corner of the view was the principal access to the marsh from the village.

Wernffrwd

East of Llanrhidian the landscape changes distinctly. This is accounted for in part by the geological change from limestone to millstone grit and the coal measures. It is also affected by the dominance of Welsh characteristics in the pattern of settlement and farming. This would have been far more marked two centuries or more ago when the villages of the upper division had not developed. The traveller would then have been aware that he was entering an area of individual farms with irregular fields - until Loughor or Swansea was reached there would be little in the way of villages or even hamlets. Wernffrwd is, therefore, an exception in such a landscape and might be best seen as a farming community which never quite matured into a village. Watered by an excellent stream - the Wernffrwd (literally 'the stream from the wern'), there was some good arable land here cleared from the woodlands of oak and hazel which are still predominant in the local hedgerows. In a transaction of 1315 there were seven landowners in the Wernffrwd area of whom at least four were Welsh. The English farmers were clearly interspersed with the Welsh in what appear to have been strips in at least one common field. We might guess that there were at least four farms making up the settlement and the obvious site for the common fields would have been to the east of the stream. On the map of the hamlet at about 1840 the vestiges of this common field are suggested by the landshares and the rhandir, once part of a larger field that would have extended across the adjacent 'Three Acres'. Further east, the hedgerow dates and alignments strongly suggest that very early enclosure had taken place there also. The manuscript of 1315 also mentions a weir; this would have been a fish trap on the sands. At that date the estuary sands extended right up to the line of the present 'Marsh Road'. On the map opposite, the farms of John Dunn (1), Mary Phillips (2) and William Williams (3) may well have been on the site of late medieval farms. Additional farms were on the Marsh Road and at Bank Farm a little further up the hill.

A gap of nearly 300 years between 1315 and the next direct reference to the settlement means that we can can only guess at how the area had developed in the intervening period. By 1594 George Lleison was established at Banc Farm - this was a period when there are records of sizeable enclosures taking place in the hinterland of Wernffrwd. Also about this time there are records of coal mines working irregularly around the hamlet and there are visible remains of some 'crop-holes' on the little hill above the west bank of the stream, these may date from some early endeavours in mining. It is likely that there were some more substantial workings close to Cae Inner ('Cae Joiner' on some old maps) and a survey of 1665 makes reference to workings on the marsh. Apart from this limited industrial activity there was probably little that had changed since the 14th century. Essentially, there was roughly the same number of farmers as in 1315; the sites of their farms, if not the buildings themselves, were probably the same. It is this likelihood that makes it probable that the reconstructed map of 1840, based on the tithe map, usefully indicates the nature of the medieval settlement. Since then, changes have been only limited. The lane along which the farms were

The farm of John Dunn in 1840 still stands today at the bottom end of the village.

established now appears to be little more than a side road off the present main road constructed in the 1930's. A number of residential buildings have been built along the lane this century whilst, in the latter half of the last century, a short terrace was built just back from the foreshore. This is reputed to be the site of the 'Flying Dolphin', the local public house. Close by, the chapel of St David was also built by the Crofty mason, David Thomas, in 1896.

The main road, built in the first half of the 20th century, cuts through the fields of Cae Tommy, Cae Santers and Easter Close in a way that has completely altered the aspect of the community. From being a quiet lane with a few farms it has developed into a residential community branching off from the main road to Swansea.

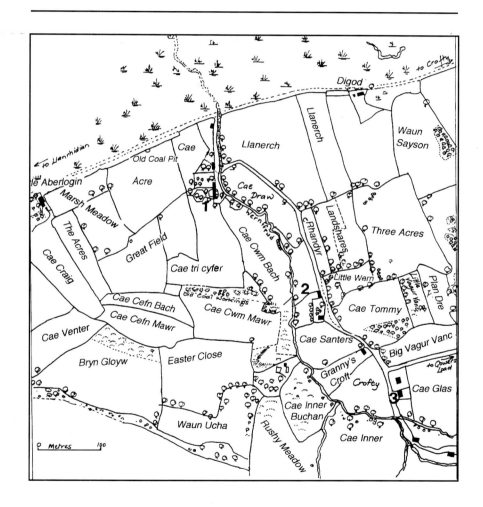

Wernffrwyd c1840.
Still little more than a collection of farms. Cae Cwm Mawr and Acre Field by the marsh, however, were the scene of some mining activity. Today's main road passes through Granny's Croft.

Crofty and Llanmorlais

The fact that no records have survived of Crofty and Llanmorlais from before the late Tudor period cannot preclude the possibility that there was settlement in this area long before that time. One cannot envisage such settlement looking anything like a village or even a hamlet in pre-Tudor times; the Celtic pattern of settlement in dispersed farms persisted in the higher part of Llanrhidian's parish right up to the beginning of the 18th century. References to place names before 1700 are almost invariably to farms or mills and not to groups of houses, let alone villages. In seeking the origins of communities such as Crofty and Llanmorlais, therefore, we must look for the original farms that were the genesis of the villages. Fortunately, these origins are still discernible and, in some cases, the buildings are still in existence.

Crofty is first mentioned in a survey of 1583. The entry reads - *'David Robert Hopkin tenet cert' terr apud Crofte, et reddit p annum iiijd. ob.'* (David Robert Hopkin holds land at Crofty and pays rent 4d per year) This follows an entry shortly before - *'David Robert Hopkin tenet ptem terr dicti Thome [ap Ievan Gwynne] apud Pen grevenny et reddit p ann ijs. iiijd.'* (David Robert Hopkin holds part of the lands of the said Thomas at Pencaerfenni and pays rent 2s 4d per year). We have met David Robert Hopkin before (see *'A New Era'*) through his detailed will dated 1596. He was the relatively wealthy farmer of Pencaerfenni whose lands seemed to extend over a considerable area to the south of the village. It would appear that Pencaerfenni was one of the 'seeds' from which the village grew. The name 'Crofte' is, perhaps, a further clue to the origins of the village. Situated on the edge of the enclosed fields of Pencaerfenni, it is likely that a number of labourers or tenants might have established smallholdings, or crofts, in the area just west of today's 'Zoar' chapel. These crofts, as they were known, would have consisted each of a small field and a little cottage which was possibly of one room only. The earliest maps suggest

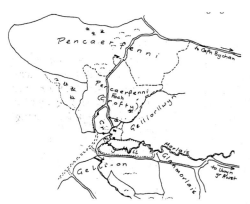

The rough extent of the farms that comprised the area around Crofty in about 1600.

*The **Crofty Inn** was originally the farmhouse central to the farming community of the area.*

that three or four such crofts had been established. In time the wide extent of the Pencaerfenni lands became broken up. For example, in the eighteenth century a distinction was made between Pencaerfenni and 'Pencaerfenni Fach', the latter being farmed by Hopkin Long in 1745. This seems to be a clear case of the breaking up of a single holding. The extent of Pencaerfenni Fach, as it became apparent by the end of the century, was synonomous with what came to be known as Crofty Farm whose central building is now the Crofty Inn. In the will and ensuing disposal of lands following the death of David Robert Hopkin in 1600 it is clear that land a good way south of the Morlais stream belonged to Hopkin, including the remains of the old farm known variously as 'Kyngy', 'Kengie', 'Kynky' or 'Cincee'. These lands came to comprise a third farm known as Gelli-on, first mentioned in 1722. In addition, there was the Crofty mill which, in 1624, belonged to the estate of Evan David Robert, the successor of David Robert Hopkin. The origin of this mill has been discussed in an earlier chapter but is likely to have been part of the Tudor origins of this community.

Pencaerfenni and its neighbouring lands belonged to the manor of Weobley although they are not mentioned as being within the stated 'bounds' of that manor. It is probable that the Crofty area was a later acquisition of Weobley, an acquisition that may date from the early Tudor rejuvenation of the manor. It may well be that the first clearance and enclosure of the area was associated with its acquisition at that time.

The 'Crofty' farms straddled the mouth of the Morlais stream, the length of which ran through dense woods and, lower in its course, the farms which made up 'Glanmorlais'. Glanmorlais, meaning 'the bank of the Morlais', receives its earliest surviving mention in documents in 1601. In the following years manuscripts refer to 'Glasmorleys', 'Abermorles', 'Morlas', 'Llanmorlies' and several other approximations to the present name of 'Llanmorlais'. Rather like Penclawdd, over the hill, the area had not yet reached the stage of fixing upon a definite name or even a precise location. But the sense of the names is clear - they refer to the community inhabiting the lower Morlais valley. By and large, this community comprised a number of small farmsteads such as Tyrgill (now ploughed out), Cwm Farm (now in ruins), Llwyn yr awst (a lost medieval farmstead) and possibly a small farm centred on present day Llanmorlais Farm. There are signs, on either side of the lowest half mile of the stream, of narrower strip fields such as Cae Gwennith through which the public footpath leads up to the Wern. This gives the impression that there may have been some communal farming and even one or two common fields in the community's earliest days. For both Llanmorlais and Crofty there was, from late Tudor times, a need for labour in the small mines operating on the Wern and at the marsh edge. Such labour would need local housing and traces of such houses are numerous enough along the lane that led up the Morlais valley towards Llwynyrawst. These took the form of encroachments along the wayside at points where it widened sufficently to permit the construction of a little cott and a surrounding plot. Some of the smaller crofts or fields could also accommodate a cottage or two together with enough land for the labourer to be tolerably self-sufficient. In spite of this the communities grew very slowly - in 1869

Some of Crofty's late 19th century houses built around the Crofty meadow, mostly for colliers in the rapidly developing mining community

Llanmorlais railway station, built in 1884, gave an added impetus to the growth of the village.

Crofty as it was about 1850. Note the Crofty Meadow (1), Crofty Farm (2) - now the Crofty Inn, Gelli-on Farm (3), Talbot's mine (4) with the tramroad (5) to a quay near Pencaerfenni, Crofty Mill (6), Pencaerfenni Farm (7), the road to the Rallt and Gower's Load (8).

Crofty was described as comprising '6 thatched cottages and 1 tiled belonging to the farm'. At this stage, Llanmorlais consisted of just 3 cottages and the Llanmorlais Farm. But the railway was on the way and in 1867, 4 years after it arrived in Penclawdd, land in Crofty was being acquired by David Thomas, a Penclawdd mason. In 1885 he made the vital acquisition of the Crofty Meadow. In the following years this field was parcelled and developed. Little houses, 9m x 5m, were erected at a cost of around £150 each and a small mining village developed around the old meadow. A similar development took place along what was now Station Road in Llanmorlais where a lengthy terrace was erected at about the same time. The first shop arrived in 1886 and, by 1911, Llanmorlais also had a Post Office. The two villages went on to boast haberdashers and shoe shops as well as general stores.

Crofty has since been the subject of very considerable development, particularly on the lands between the Crofty Farm (which in about 1880 became the Crofty Inn) and the Pencaerfenni Farm. A sort of ribbon development of private and corporation houses has linked the two farms whilst their fields have been built over by the sprawling Pencaerfenni

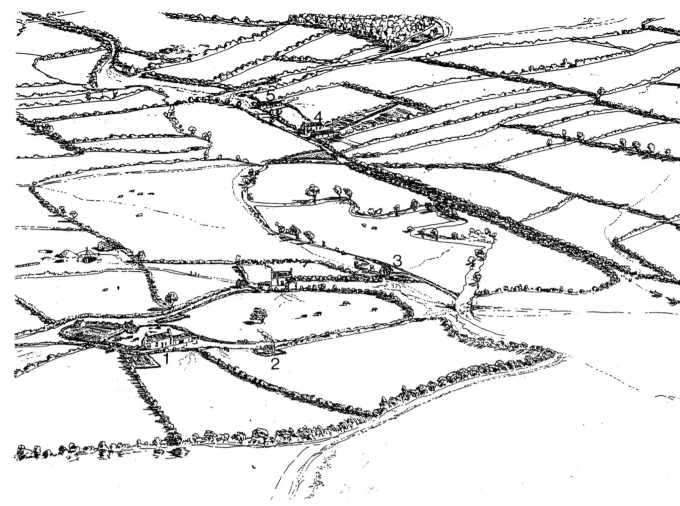

and Rhydyfenni estates. The site of the old Gelli-on farmyard has been developed into 'Hazel Tree Copse', a cul-de-sac of Georgian style houses. Smaller developments have affected Llanmorlais, the little 'Riverside' development by the lower Morlais stream, 'Trem y Mor' on the edge of the old Kyngy farmlands and some modest infill along Station Road. But in both Crofty and Llanmorlais the historic, rural feel of the communities has been virtually eradicated.

Looking towards Llanmorlais about 1850. In the foreground is the Crofty Farm (1) and the the forge (2). A path led past the Crofty Mill (3) across the fields to Llanmorlais which then consisted of little more than cottages (4) housing fishermen and colliers and the Llanmorlais Farm (5) still intact today.

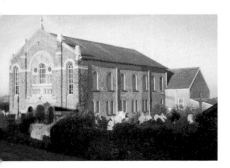

Crwys Farm - one of the key sites from which the village grew.

Three Crosses

Three Crosses occupies the highest part of the ridge that runs from Penclawdd to Dunvant at the eastern end of the parish. The present village sprawls across an area much greater than the original settlement and also encompasses the area round Poundffald in the west. Indeed, the modern 1:25000 Ordnance Survey map goes so far as to place the name 'Three Crosses' by that western part of the village at quite the opposite end to the part for which, until recently, that name was reserved. To understand this settlement at all, we have to go back at least 500 years to when the Welsh pattern of dispersed settlement was still dominant in the area. In Tudor times a settlement would not have been recognisable beyond the fact that there were some farms in the area. Of these, the two most ancient were Rhean Farm, to the north, and Killan Farm to the east. Both farms were mentioned in deeds of the 14th century. There was also an area belonging to the priory of Llangennith, possibly a farm, the memory of which is preserved in the name 'Prior's Meadow' to the south east (on the northern edge of Fairwood Common). One theory concerning the origin of the name 'Three Crosses' relates it to this monastic holding which may have been marked by crosses on its boundary.

In the post-medieval period other farms were established in the area such as Ystlys yr Rhean and Cefn Draw. Three Crosses Farm was another such farm but the name does not seem to enter common parlance until the 18th century. In a survey of 1583 reference is made to 'Bryn Croysse'; by the 17th century this was typically shortened to 'Crwys' but a survey of 1665 places one David Bennet at 'the Three Crosses'. In 1682 there is a record of encroachment by Thomas Bennet at Three Crosses - maps showing the field boundaries reveal a pattern of such encroachments southwards towards Fairwood Common and it may be at this time that the farm was established through this process. The present building of Three Crosses Farm (now called 'Crwys Farm') is a structure of about 1800 and was built at the point where the lane from Dunvant forked. The northerly track continued westward along the ridge and on to Penclawdd, the southerly route descended over what must have been open moor or common land to follow the ridge marking the south side of the Morlais valley. This route would have led, eventually, to Llanrhidian with lesser tracks descending to Llanmorlais and Wernffrwd. All that is left of the open moor is the triangular green between the 'Pavilion' and Crwys Chapel. At Three Crosses farm the old ridgeway also joined, or crossed, a track leading to Aberwassa (Gowerton) to the north. The 'ridgeway' track used to run north of the 'Pavilion'. There is a local feeling that the name 'Three Crosses' relates to crossroads and that this junction would have been one of them. The other two crosses would have been where the Penclawdd and Llanrhidian tracks both had to cross an ancient track which used to run in an almost straight line from Bishopston to Rhean (Fawr) and possibly on to Cefnstylle. The lower cross was at Tirymynnydd and the higher at Poundffald. The origin of the the name Poundffald is, happily, still apparent. The present Poundfold Inn preserves, as part of its structure, the original, circular,

Capel-y-Crwy – built in 1876 to a design by John Humphrey, architect of Tabernacle, Morriston

60

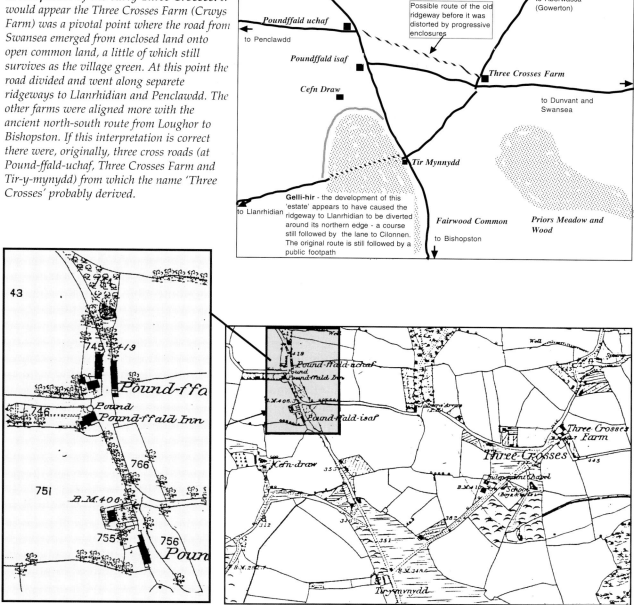

A map showing the main features in the development of the early Three Crosses. It would appear the Three Crosses Farm (Crwys Farm) was a pivotal point where the road from Swansea emerged from enclosed land onto open common land, a little of which still survives as the village green. At this point the road divided and went along separete ridgeways to Llanrhidian and Penclawdd. The other farms were aligned more with the ancient north-south route from Loughor to Bishopston. If this interpretation is correct there were, originally, three cross roads (at Pound-ffald-uchaf, Three Crosses Farm and Tir-y-mynydd) from which the name 'Three Crosses' probably derived.

The 1878 Ordnance Survey map shows that, even at that date there was very little development of the area. Note that the farm 'Pound-ffald-uchaf' was still standing and the road to Swansea at Three Crosses farm took a sharp 'Z' bend before aligning with the road we use today. The inset shows Pound-ffald-uchaf on a larger scale, revealing that in 1878 the old pound was still a separate and unroofed structure, technically still in use.

61

stone pound in which stray animals were kept on behalf of the manor court (see 'Llanrhidian at Court').

Parts of Three Crosses belonged to the manor of Weobley but the pound was in the manor of Subboscus. This we know from a record in the Badminton Court books dated 1691 which records that George William *'broke the common pound at Three Crosses to bring out his mare, put in the common pound by John Hinton for trespass'*. These same court books indicate the activity developing around Three Crosses at the time. In 1712 there was an instruction that coal pits *'dugged on Fairwood common'* should be filled-in. In 1742 William Benbow, a Penclawdd man, was mining on the lands of Gellihir whilst Robert Morris was digging pits on Fairwood Common. In 1755 a wagonway was built on Mynydd Bach (probably Mynydd Bach y Cocs) in Llanrhidian. This was for the carrying of coals from local mines - clearly the area had a burgeoning coal industry. And yet, by the time of the mid-nineteenth century when the first detailed maps of the area were produced, Three Crosses was still little more than a cluster of farms. Close to Three Crosses Farm, around the green which was known as 'Bank y Crwys Common', were half a dozen cottages and the Crwys Chapel. Around the farms of Cefn Draw, Pumfallt and Pumfallt Issa a few more cottages are marked. Together with Tirymynydd Farm this really marks the sum total of the community.

The chapel at Crwys, whose history was admirably traced by Wyn Jones in 1988, had its origins in one of the oldest non-conformist communities in Wales. From the time of the 17th century persecutions, the farmhouse of Cwmmawr had been used for services by a congregation of non-conforming churchgoers of eastern Gower. A church was built close to the farm, possibly as early as 1689 but, when the lease ran out, a new church was erected at Crwys on the site of the present Crwys chapel. This took place in 1788. Since then there have been rebuildings on a larger scale and the original chapel would not have had such an imposing presence as it now has. (See also 'Llanrhidian Worships')

The 25 inch map of 1878 reveals that most building in the village in the third quarter of the nineteenth century was taking place on the road to Gowerton which, together with Waunarlwydd and Dunvant, was outstripping the mining industry in the parish of Llanrhidian. The Gellihir and Killan collieries were, however, active during this period. By 1878 the 'Joiner's Arms' stood astride the road between Three Crosses and Poundffald. The map also shows a saw pit almost opposite the front door of the house, suggesting not only the origin of the name but also a significant part of its custom. The growing community also had its own school by this time and continued to expand into the next century. In 1911 a Post Office was established and by 1920 there were some 60 houses spread around the triangle of roads. After the Second World War, however, expansion went into another gear and the whole of the inside part of the 'triangle' was developed with private and corporation housing.

With three crossroads and as many potential centres, Three Crosses has remained an 'uncentred' village. The real reason for this lies in its distant origins not as a village but as a loose cluster of farms and labourers' cottages.

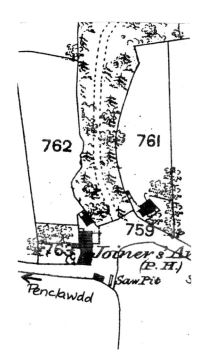

In 1878 the 'Joiners' was approached rather differently by the roads from Swansea and Penclawdd which passed to the south of the building. Note the sawpit frim which, presumably, the public house gained its name. Reproduced from the 1879 Ordnance Survey map.

Penclawdd

The origins of Penclawd are as obscure as any part of the history of Llanrhidian parish. Considering that it is by far the largest community in the parish, higher and lower, it is particularly strange that it is one of the latest entrants onto the stage of recorded local history. The earliest reference that this writer has found is in the will of 1647 (written in 1646) of Philip John who bequeathed to his wife, Elizabeth, *'those two messuages called upper pen Clawth and the Lower pen clawth'*. There is a fleeting mention in a Cromwellian survey of 1650; thirteen years later a 'Thomas Griffith of Penclauth' left his will. There is one earlier reference in the records of genealogies, the 'Limbus Patrum', to William Morgan of Penclawdd in 1585 but this cannot be regarded as a primary source. How can it be, we wonder, that Crofty, Llanmorlais and even Three Crosses are recorded before this major (in the context of a rural parish) settlement warranted any mention at all?

Lying on the dark, north, side of a hill in the most Welsh part of the parish it is reasonable to suppose that here, more than anywhere else, the pattern of dispersed settlement was prevalent until pressures of a non-agricultural nature brought about the formation of a village. The difficulty is that much of the original farmland was built over before adequate maps and records of the village were made. Clues do exist, however, and in discussing these it is to be hoped that something of the village's early history can be revealed. The earliest farms in the area of which we have mention are Abercedi (1581), Penylan (1521), Hendy (1581) and Cefnbychan. The dates are the earliest at which a reference is found to a particular farm. Cefnbychan, perhaps the oldest farm, has no mention until the 17th century but the neighbouring chapel at Llanyrnewydd is known to date from Tudor times at least; in addition the field patterns and other contextual clues all point to Cefnbychan being a settlement of medieval origins.

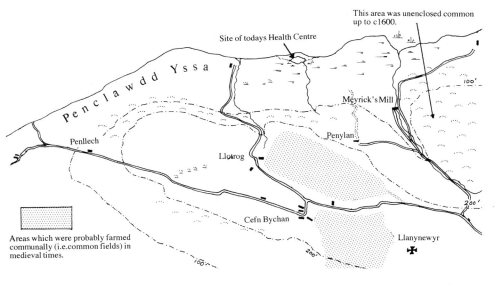

This area was unenclosed common up to c1600.

Site of todays Health Centre

Penclawdd Yssa

Meyrick's Mill

Penllech

Penylan

Llotrog

Cefn Bychan

Llanynewyr

Areas which were probably farmed communally (i.e.common fields) in medieval times.

The origins of Penclawdd. The principle farms in the area at the time of the 16th and 17th centuries.

63

The following pages present a reconstruction of Penclawdd as it looked along its waterfront around 1840-50. They make most sense if the reader imagines these pictures as the view seen by a seaman aboard a vessel leaving the copper works and going downstream towards Burry Port and the sea.

The first picture depicts the copper works (see pages 69 ff) and the entrance to the dock. At this time the works were being revived as a result of the interest of the Benson family. The original lead works - 'The Kent House' - are to the left. The sluice gate from the inner pond can just be seen behind the stern of the vessel in the dock.

In addition to these farms there were, by 1646, the farms called 'Penclauth' in Philip John's will. On his death in January, 1647, a quarter of the value of the farms was in corn, the rest in livestock. Where these farms were is difficult to say and there seems to have been some dispute in the following century as to their boundaries. A manuscript, dated 1732, held in the National Library of Wales's Penrice and Margam collection (no. 2666) contains a deposition by four working men of the area as to the extent of 'Penclawdd Yssa'. These four men cast their minds back to 1684 and beyond, when lower Penclawdd was part of Weobley Manor. Unfortunately for us, the extent was marked mostly by a series of thorn bushes and a limekiln of which nothing can be traced today. It is, however, plain that lower Penclawdd was adjacent to Pencaerfenni's lands on its western side. We might guess that on the east it reached as far as the present day Tabernacle Chapel. This deposition also records their memories of ships coming up the river to lie on the 'wast or strand in Penclawdd Yssa' and of the cutting of oak trees around Pencaerfenni.

A further clue also comes to us from a survey made in 1688 of part of the manor of Knelston to which belonged a narrow swathe of land running south from the present Post Office as far as Coldharbour Farm near Cefnbychan. This survey refers to Penclawdd as an alternative name to Cefnbychan. Having established that lower Penclawdd pertains to the area along the edge of the estuary towards Pencaerfenni's lands it seems reasonable to suppose that the old settlement of Cefnbychan was also known as higher Penclawdd. The name 'Penclawdd' (lit. 'point of the ditch') clearly relates to the old Celtic earthworks on the hill at Penygaer and may well have been the original name for the hill itself since it is such

a dominant feature, both from the estuary and further away. It is not unusual for names of hills or streams to be lost, in this case we may guess that the name has become subsumed in a name that stood for a whole area and for at least one of its farms.

There may seem to be at this stage a rather tenuous framework for describing the area as it was at about 1600 - perhaps a half dozen farms the exact siting of which is not clear. The general proposition that this was the appearance of the area is, however, one that can be made with some confidence. Such concentration of settlement as there was would probably have been around Cefnbychan which was at the centre of a group of landshares and small enclosures. In the period up to 1700 it is clear that the name Penclawdd became detached from either the hill or the farm of that name and became applied to a new cluster of buildings developing near the shore of the estuary. Why did this cluster of buildings develop? The answer to this question, at least, is beyond doubt - coal. As mining grew in importance in the area there was a demand for workers both in the mines and in the business of getting the coal into ships. Penclawdd was far and away the most convenient point in the parish for loading coal into vessels and a permanent population of labourers was required for this task as well as for its being overseen. The traditional site for the shipping offices is said to be in Beach Cottage adjacent to today's 'Royal Oak'. This was close to the point where the lane from Cefnbychan reached the foreshore. It appears that the road which, at present, runs from Caban Isaac diagonally across the hillside down to the foreshore at the 'Royal Oak' was constructed in the latter half of the 18th century. This meant that prior to the late 18th century the Cefnbychan lane was the only one which gave access to the lower part of the village.

Leaving the tidal dock the end of the tramway from the Penclawdd colliery can be seen. Coal was loaded into waiting vessels at this point. The colliery is up on the hill (1) not far from the old Penlan Farm (2) which has long since disappeared. The little track leading from Penlan down to the foreshore is still used today, descending past the old 'Collier's Arms' (3), the quarry (4) and what was to be the 'Swn y Mor' (5) in the field lower down. The tramway from the colliery enabled coal to be delivered to the quay for shipping as well as to the copper works.

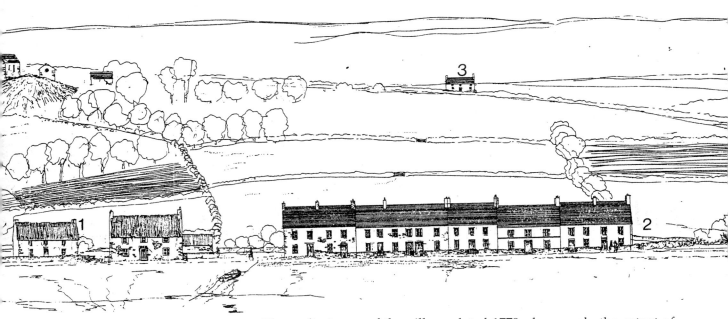

Near the site of the present chemists shop and 'Min y dwr' were two thatched houses. That on the left (1) has a doorplate surviving showing that it was built in 1765 for David and Mary Lewis - innkeepers in Penclawdd. The row of cottages to the right was in existence by 1779 and still stands today with additions on either end. Today's Post Office is one of those later additions. (2) On the hill can be seen 'Emlyn Cottage' (3).

The earliest map of the village, dated 1779, shows only the extent of the Knelston manor lands which were now part of the Dunraven estate. It is clear, however, that by this date the village was more substantial. At the east end was a new brass works and, close by, adjacent to today's Post Office, was a row of cottages whose fabric forms part of the same row of cottages on the site now. On the site of today's Health Centre are shown more substantial houses with front gardens. In front of these gardens was a pond, probably a relic of a little lagoon by the estuary, which is still remembered by a few villagers. There were cottages, too, by the new turnpike road which had radically improved the route down to the foreshore from 'upper Penclawdd' by cutting a straight road with a steady, if steep, gradient. The old route down from Llotrog had tortuous twists and alarming gradients which would have made the carriage of coal a difficult task. The lane, now little more than a footpath for most of its length, that ran from Banc Bach above what was to be Bethel Chapel seems to have become a focus for colliers cottages. They were small thatched roof affairs, a few of which survived into the present century. They were built where the land was too steep to work and therefore of little economic value, thus making them cheap to establish. When Starling Benson built the village's first school the site he chose was Banc Bach, on the turnpike road.

More substantial houses were built closer to the foreshore in the vicinity of today's Tabernacle Chapel. The road along here, leading on towards Crofty came to be known as known as 'Water Street', doubtless because at high tide the Crofty end was submerged. Here, in the nineteenth century, lived retired army captains and mariners as well as colliers and metal workers. The 'Pink Cottages' still standing in West End, as that part of the village is now known, may be a survival from the late 18th century. In the early part of the 19th century they were adjacent

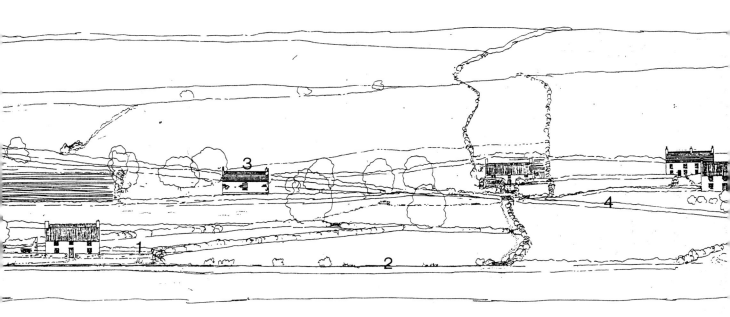

to the shipbuilding yard of Howell John. The hulls of substantial schooners would have stood well above the roofline of these little cottages. On the seaward (north) side of Water Street, at this time, there were no houses at all.

Sadly, there are few survivals from before the latter part of the 19th century. The 'Pink Cottages' have been mentioned, so also 'Beach Cottage' adjacent to the 'Royal Oak' public house. The cottages adjacent to the Post Office may also, in part, be survivals from workers' housing of the late 18th century. Of more substantial houses there remains 'The Lodge', built c1820. In 1847 it belonged to the Morris estate and was let to Starling Benson - part owner of the copper works. A reference in 1823 to 'Penclawdd Lodge', residence of Alexander Prole, captain of the 83rd regiment of foot, is likely to be the same building which has the internal evidence of a small Regency house. The house occupied part of a field between the foreshore road and the cottages of Banc Bach and represents a period when some infilling of the farmland between the beach and the hillslope was beginning in the village. More substantial but of similar style and date is the house now known as 'Tanglewood' but until relatively recently known as 'Brynhir'. Overlooking the higher part of the village this house was built by the Evans family, farmers of the adjacent Brynhir Farm and of Pencaerfenni. It represented the pinnacle of domestic architecture in the village and was lived in, during the latter part of the 19th century, by the pinnacle of its society - Mr J Baker Haynes.

A well known photograph of the village, taken about 1900, shows two large cottages, thatched-roofed, close to the site of the present-day chemist shop by the foreshore. There is evidence that one of these was built in 1765 and was kept as an inn. The other cottage is likely to be of similar date. The construction of such buildings is likely to have related

On the site of today's health centre (1) was a small cluster of ruins together with a small cottage and garden. Next to these was a large pond (2) - now the site of the village's 'memorial gardens'. On the hillside at Banc Bach, Starling Benson was to erect the school (3) in 1843. The turnpike road (4) ran down past the school towards the heart of the old village (next page).

The 'Coasting Pilot' (1) public house - here behind a building on the sea front - was one of the earliest drinking houses in the village. The track from here to Llotrog ran steeply up the hill with cottages all along its length. 'Bethel' chapel (2) was first built in 1816 and is seen here in its original form with Barham house adjacent. 'The Lodge' (3), built shortly after, was a large house occupied principally by managers of the metal works. Half of the reputed shipping office (4) still stands in the form of 'Beach Cottage', the other half being now occupied by 'The Royal Oak' public house.

to the copper works which were established prior to 1779 and quite probably as early as 1760.

In addition to these buildings, the area north of Penlan Farm also developed a small cluster of cottages doubtless connected with the Penclawdd Colliery which operated throughout the nineteenth century. To the east, below Penlan, was the venerable Meyrick's Mill which was working up to the 1880's. Blue Anchor, first mentioned in 1796, is shown on the tithe map of c1847 as a group of three cottages. It seems most probable that the name should come from the public house, and not vice-versa. The tithe map describes the site of the inn as 'cottage and garden' but in the Cambrian of 1844 (22nd June) it is advertised as a 'well frequented public house.......John Harris vict.' .

It may seem strange that the centre of Penclawdd today would appear to be a half mile east of most of the central points in the last century. It was the arrival of the railway in 1863 followed by the erection of the tinplate works in 1872 that led to a concentration of building and services at the eastern end of the village. Bellevue Terrace, for example, was built around 1881, just before Station Terrace. But the old village kept some of the principle services - all the chapels, most of the public houses; even the Post Office, which had arrived in 1853, continued to be maintained in the village's main shop - the Compton House Emporium.

The Penclawdd Metalworks

In the 18th century, any place in the kingdom with coal seams close to a navigable waterway was likely to be considered for the establishment of a metalworks. Since it took three tons of coal to smelt one of copper, it clearly made sense to bring the copper to the coal rather than vice-versa. Wages were relatively low in south Wales and this additional factor made the Swansea area attractive to entrepreneurs in this market. As early as

1729, Penclawdd was considered as a site for a copper works. This proposal, in the words of Robert Morris, 'came to nothing' but, in the latter half of the century metal smelting and processing was certainly taking place at Penclawdd.

The Dunraven Estate map of 1779 shows a brass works in Penclawdd. In his definitive note on the early history of the works, R O Roberts suggests that a Mr Dagley was closely involved in the work of the plant. The late Mr Nyall Davies asserted that Mr Dagley was in the village as early as 1772 and this date could accord well with the initial establishment of the works. Certainly, by the late 1780's we have records of copper arriving from Anglesey as well as lead from St Clears and Cardigan. At this time the works belonged to one of the Anglesey copper companies but later it came into the hands of the Cheadle Brass Wire Company and the chief supplies of copper came from Cornwall. It was the Cornish connection that brought John Vivian, one of Swansea's most noted industrialists, to Penclawdd. R O Roberts has shown that during this early period the Penclawdd works produced, among other things, copper or bronze items that could be used in the purchase of slaves as part of the notorious 'triangular trade' between Britain, West Africa and the Americas.

The copper works was always a small concern, probably not employing above 30 men. The value of the works to Penclawdd and its area was, however, much greater. As long as the works were operating, coal was required from local mines and the coal hewers were guaranteed employment. There was work, also, in the port of Penclawdd, unloading vessels of ore and copper, loading them with coal for a return cargo, repairing and victualling vessels, and overseeing the customs arrangements. But the works generally remained at the margins of viability of the copper industry - processing low grade ores and handling relatively small quantities. Much of the work was in processing already

The 'Ship and Castle' (1) was a major feature of the sea front with a little green in front that was used by church members of 'Tabernacle' before they built their church in 1836. 'The Park' (2) behind the inn became the site of the school in the 20th century. The turnpike road reached the foreshore (3) by the 'Ship and Castle' but the original 'main road' to Penclawdd reached the same spot from the other side of the inn (4). 'Compton House' (5) became a major emporium for the village next to the venerable 'George Inn (6).

Earlier coalworks already scarred the village in 1840 as at 'Hafod y Gan' (1). The first 'Tabernacle' (2) was a modest building with the minister's

smelted ores. Should any misfortune befall the industry in general, a marginal plant, such as that at Penclawdd, would be the first to 'feel the pinch'. Around 1808 the works were beset by the twin ills of bad management and failing coal supplies. Although both problems were capable of remedy (there were ample supplies of coal across the estuary at Loughor and Llanelli) the profitability of the works was, nonetheless, jeopardised. By 1823 we find the works closed and little prospect of their resuming production. Having built up a certain dependence on them, we must surmise that this was a period of great economic difficulty for the village.

The Benson family began to acquire land in Penclawdd from 1826 onwards - initially developing the Penclawdd Colliery but also, about 1839, the metal works. Financial difficulties followed during which the works were taken over by Charles Low. The surviving archway has an entablature marked 'L.P.C.C. 1848' - the Low Patent Copper Company. The works, in order to survive, clearly had to diversify. When Low ran into financial difficulties the Benson family took over the ownership in 1850. The works later passed through various hands and uses before their closure at the turn of the century.

The tinplate works came to Penclawdd somewhat similarly to the copper works a century earlier. Tinplate was a booming industry in the mid-nineteenth century and the Burry Estuary its epi-centre. The works established in Penclawdd in 1872 by Herbert Llewelyn Morris were, however, peripheral to the main operations being carried on and, like the copper works, were vulnerable to small difficulties and variations in the market. For example, the low wages paid in Wales remained one of the attractions for entrepreneurial ventures of this kind; when these wages were challenged by the workforce, within two years of the works opening, their future was called into question and closure followed. A pattern of opening and closure followed over the next 20 years. When the

works were closed we may assume that the village was in a depressed state but when they were open, alongside the copper works, with a new railway arrived in the village and local mines flourishing, Penclawdd must have seemed on the verge of a great leap forward. It was a leap that a little village like Gorseinon took, subsequently becoming a real town. Penclawdd never seems to have crossed that threshold; when the metal works staggered towards final closure in the years either side of the turn of the century Penclawdd was relapsing from a period of relatively frenetic industrial activity and was never to recover. Although the mines continued to be active for some years it can be said that the village was among the first parts of Wales to be blighted by depression and loss of employment that cursed the rest of the country later in the twentieth century.

This account of the metal works in Penclawdd is very much a condensing of a complex story that is described in greater detail in R O Robert's articles in the Gower Journals numbers 5 and 14 and also in R N Cooper's 'A Dark and Pagan Place'. A great deal of new light has, however, been cast on the complex story by D Bayliss and J Harding in their definitive volume 'Starling Benson of Swansea' (1996).

Coal 1650 - 1800

The earliest mining activities in the parish were, as we have seen already, carried out by small syndicates of farmers or local landowners. We have been able to locate precisely the central point of one of the earliest syndicates, headed by the farmer of Pencaerfenni, in the fields below Penllwynrobert Farm around the period 1590 to 1620. During the 17th century, merchants and entrepreneurs from Swansea and further afield became more and more interested in developing the potential of the higher end of Llanrhidian's parish. Increasingly it was seen that here

Glanymor Farm (1) was clearly one of the original buildings of Penclawdd, now sadly lost. The 'Pink Cottages' (2) are, however, still standing. At this time there were no buildings on the seaward side of the road. This part of the village street was known as 'Water Street'.

71

Beyond the 'Pink Cottages'(1) was Howell John's shipyard (2) which built its last vessel in 1838. 'The Hall' (3), adjacent to the shipyard, was probably a building of some significance in the village although falling into some disrepair at the time. Coed Farm (4) was a humble building, the remains of which can still just be seen on the edge of today's Graig y Coed estate.

were good seams of coal outcropping close to a navigable waterway which made it all the easier to find a market for the product. In the earliest days it was easy to obtain leases of land on terms highly advantageous to the mining company. William Basset, for example, payed just £20 a year in 1665 for the right to mine coal. As landowners realised that there was money in mining they became increasingly encouraging to potential operators. They began to charge on the basis of the amount of coal extracted from their land at rates of between (approximately) 2p and 10p a ton. A productive mine like the Wern was, in 1689, able to produce something like 4000 tons of coal. This is based on the figure of 2637 'weys' of coal according to the account for that year. The amount of a 'wey' is open to conjecture and caused much disputation at the time but the most likely measure in our area was the 'Gower wey' - approximately one and a half tons. Even on the smallest allowable levy by the landowner it can be seen that a healthy dividend could be reaped from his land for next to no effort at all.

The earliest mines were all in the area between Wernffrwd and Cilonnen. The survey of Landimore in 1665 records that there were *'colemines within ye lords comon or wast in ye marshes neere to Loughor River, wch mine is now out of work ...'*. The low lying land at the edge of the estuary was the scene of some of the earliest and the latest coal operations in the parish - an operation always fraught with danger from flooding. In later years the miners would tell of being able to hear the waters of the estuary above their heads. The westerly limit of coal outcropping above ground in Gower was on the boundary between the higher and lower divisions of Llanrhidian at a little field by the estuary called 'The Lynch'. Whether this field gave its name to the seam or vice-versa it is difficult to say but it was a seam that was to be thoroughly exploited from the Clyne Valley and Blackpill all the way to its watery termination under the marshes of Llanrhidian. The works in this area made Wernffrwd one of the most active areas of mining outside Swansea during the latter part of the 17th century. In 1668 Llyson Price was operating around the hamlet, probably near the Lynch field but also in fields close to the Wernffrwd stream. On the little hill just west of the stream and above the present village are scars of mining works that follow the line of the Lynch seam.

It is probable that local people took advantage of the coal seams for their personal use throughout this early period. Remains of crop holes, the simplest and most primitive excavation of coal close to the surface, can still be seen stretching across the hillside north of the old 'Hermon Chapel'. These excavations would have informed developers with more ambitious plans and gradually the scene of operations extended northwards across Graig Penclawdd and Llanyrnewydd and on towards Berthlwyd. According to one authority (W. Rees - 1968) Berthlwyd was also the scene of mining in the Tudor period.

Apart from these simple crop holes, coal was obtained from bell pits, slants and deep mines. Deep mines only began to be seen in the 18th century but the smaller bell pits and slants, requiring much less capital investment, were commonplace throughout the area for much of its mining history. A typical bell-pit was sunk down between 10 and 20 metres (according to records for our area) and coal was removed by working out from the base of the shaft as long as collapse, flooding or exhaustion of seams could be avoided. How long this might take is suggested by records for pits operated at Llanmorlais between 1770 and 1771 by Thomas Mansel, John Lucas and Gabriel Powell. As an example, the production in cartloads from December 1770 to September 1771 from the Lucas and Powell pits can be shown on a graph. It should be noted that 'cartloads' may be relatively small quantities since the state of roads was hardly likely to permit loads of more than half a ton at a time.

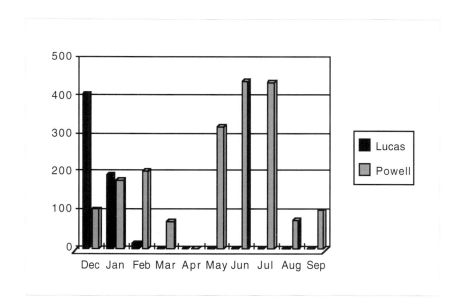

The entire life of Powell's pit can be seen here - overlapping with the end of Lucas's pit. The non-production during April is explained, in the source manuscript, by work being diverted to open a new pit. This, presumably, would be ready to start production in September or October as the production of the original pit failed. Alternatively, the figures for Powell's pit during December to March may represent a separate pit which was near exhaustion when work was begun on a new pit which came into full production in May. Either way, the life of these pits appears to be between just 4 and 9 months. The number of cartloads is shown on the left hand scale.

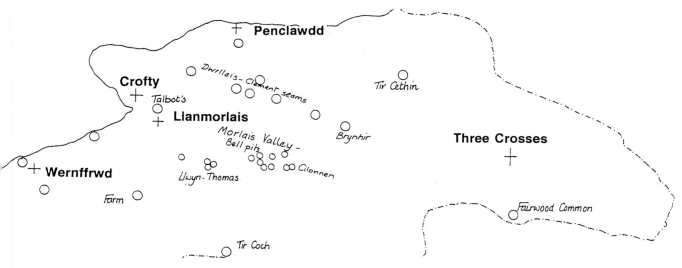

Principle mines operating between 1650 and 1750.

Facts and figures can obscure the reality of coal work which must have been a hazardous operation for the miners. Something of the flavour of the times can be gleaned from correspondence between the gentry of which just a little has survived from the early 18th century.

In this letter from the Rev. David Evans, rector of Nicholaston, who had the living of Llanrhidian parish, we see the competition for mining rights and the means by which prospective miners tried to secure advantage. The 'Widdow Price' lived at Gelli-on Farm by Crofty and claimed to hold lands around Llanyrnewydd and Brynhir. The note of obsequiousness was typical of all Evans's correspondence with his patron.
Penrice and Margam L1025

Nicholaston ffeb 6th 1722
My most honrd Lord,
This day I have had a proposal made unto me, wch I verily believe will turn to a very good account to your Lordship, the old man Wm Jones wch your Lordship sent to deal with me, will give but 3d a weigh for ye work only, now the proposal made to me is, by some already concern'd under your Lordship, to give 4d a weigh, and to be impowered to work everywhere upon your Lordship's tenement called Brynhir, held by ye Widdow Price, as I have already sgnified to your Lordship. I writ already to your Lordship of ye said widow's pretentions. She told me she wd carry her lease to your Lordship to Margam now I found her lease is at Brecon. Let it be where it will I am satisfyed she hath no right, thee persons yt are desirous to be concerned under your Lordship, will be willing to be off, if she can make good her pretentions. One thing I have to recomend to your Lordship in ye behalfe of these partners yt altho they have suffered shipwreck yet in their language are able to build once more, and if your Lordship approves of their proposal. They will forthwith go to work and would gladly know your Lordships Resolutions @ Saturday's Post which I have engaged to communicate to them if I receive ye same. I am not able to expres my joy for Mr Mansel's honour's success in ye house of Comons. wch I heard but late, may it ever be ye same to his Honour, & to all you Lordship('s) noble issue is the hearty Prayers as in Duty bound.of my most honoured Lord.
Your Lordship's most Dutiful
& most obedient humble Servant,
D.A.Evans.

Nicholaston Augt.14.1722
My most Honoured Lord,
The old man hath raised some coal upon your Lordship's lands near ye Chappel, but not of the vein he mentioned oft to your Lordship, he hath been very pressing upon me to write to yo(ur) Ldshp for an order to have a way to carry it out of ye ground ever since I returned from Carmarthenshire, but I was not willing to trouble your Lordship about it before I had seen where it lay, and what quantity he had above ground. I told him then yt I thought it not proper to write to your Ldship about it till he had such a quantity as would load a vessel , in answer to wch he sd he wanted provision &c. the trespass upon yr tenant will be but small only thro one little field and then it is in ye highway. I know not what good account you will have from yr Golden Sands my Lord, but I know there are 2 bargains there now and each raised coal, and speciall good coal it is , the best I think in all Gower.
(This letter proceeds to describe disputes between the writer and William Seys of Killan and also with Matthew Pryce)

Your Lordship's most Dutifill
& most obedient humble Servant,
D.A.Evans.

In this letter it becomes clear that the local vicar acted as business representative for many local miners who were neither literate enough nor of sufficient status to approach Lord Mansel themselves. The reference to 'ye Chappel' is to the old chapel-of-ease at Llanyrnewydd. Note the reference to shipping coal; at this period of the early 18th century all the coal was 'sent to sea' whereas in the latter half of the century most coal was distributed around Gower or used locally. The 'Golden sands' is clearly a reference to mining work in the Burry Estuary which must have been an especially hazardous operation.
Penrice and Margam L1025

Penclauth 18:7:1726
Sir
It tis evident I have been at a vast expence in driving the Level at Llanmorles which when once finished would be really a very considerable advantage to my Lord Mansell. For provided I have a grant of the old coalworks during his Lordships Minority I shall endeavour to drain it and oblige myself to pay three shillings pr weigh, which you are satisfied by Mr Bennetts Lease, is actually the Land mony I pay him.
I assure you I have the only leave(l) that can possibly be brought up to drain it, and my endeavours shant be wanting to carry it on effectually And I hope to his Lordships advantage so far that in all probability he may receive a Hundred and Fifty pound per Ann from it without any wast in the least commited upon the premisses excepting where the old workmen have been engaged in.
I expect in order to carry out the work effectually to be supplied with what coalpit timber lies commodious and convenient for the works at the customary rate they are sold in the Countrey. I must beg the favour of your result as to these proposals with the expedition imaginable and you will thereby infinitely oblige.
Your very humble servant
Matt. Pryce.

A final letter is from Matthew Pryce himself, one of the most vigorous entrepreneurs in the area. Pryce experienced a fair number of failures but was constantly on the lookout for opportunities. In the footnote to the letter Mansel's agent, Edward Hancorne, advises that there 'is no other can make a works of it but him(i.e. Pryce)'. Pryce was planning to work in Cilonnen Fawr and Cilonnen Fach - both regarded as part of Llanmorlais at that time.
Penrice and Margam L1135

The sale to sea of coal from the Llanmorlais area was thriving during the 1720's but by mid-century problems began to arise with shipping in the estuary. It is clear that captains were increasingly reluctant to risk their ships in the uncertain waters of the upper estuary and, without improvements to the navigation and shipping facilities, Llanrhidian was bound to suffer in competition with more accessible coalfields. In particular, we should bear in mind that Swansea was now able to produce coal above the lower reaches of the River Tawe, this coal could be run down to waiting vessels in a simple operation. It is likely, therefore, that Swansea money would be increasingly transferred away from Llanrhidian to concentrate on more profitable ventures close to the town. As the shipping of coal decreased, so the distribution of coal to Gower increased. This was mainly effected through the carriage of cartloads across the peninsula's notorious lanes. The worst of the hills to be negotiated by carts was likely to be that leading from the Wern up to Forest Common where a lane would have emerged on the summit near the old highway at Gower's Load. The name 'Gower's Load' may well derive from a practice of leaving coal for collection at that point for distribution across Gower.

It was not just shipping that created difficulties for the coal industry in the latter half of the eighteenth century. Severe problems were encountered with regard to flooding and gas as well. Whilst the gas could be dealt with through effective ventilation the water problem was more intractable. The geology of the area together with the natural wetness of the local climate meant that the seams were oozing water everywhere. A miner in the twentieth century described the area as like *'the Indian Ocean underground'*. In 1795 a serious accident occurred at Wernffrwd when old workings were broken into and four miners were drowned by the in-rush of water. There were also complaints about trial diggings for coal which channelled even more water into some existing workings. It is clear that some of the new 'fire engines' were being introduced into the Cilonnen mines to provide mechanical pumping but, with a decline in capital investment in favour of Swansea, it is likely that workings were abandoned as they had to pursue the seams more deeply. By the end of the first decade of the 19th century there was almost no mining activity in the area.

Higher and Lower

We have seen (*Welsh and English - the First Divide*) that, even as early as the late medieval period, differences were appearing between the different ends of the parish of Llanrhidian. These differences were based on the essentially Welsh character of the inhabitants at the eastern end and the more English nature of the western end of the parish. From the Tudor period onwards this divide became more and more institutionalised until we have, now, two quite seperate communities - Higher and Lower Llanrhidian - albeit with a common heritage.

When, in 1587, the inhabitants of 'the chapel of Llanynewyr' were given dispensation to attend services in their own community rather than travel to Llanrhidian village it was a recognition that separate communities were beginning to develop as well as of the distance between them. It was at this time that coal mining was becoming established around Llanmorlais and the area was probably beginning to show signs of population growth. Through the following century the wills of the inhabitants show an increasing, but not universal, tendency to distinguish between the lower and higher parts of the parish. This reflects that the testators wanted people whom they knew to benefit from provisions of their will and this, in turn, reflects the sense of different communities developing. Neither administration of the manor courts nor the records of the parish register reflected any division in the parish. But when taxes such as the Hearth Tax (1669-1672) were collected a distinction was made between lower and higher divisions as well as the Walterston/Cillibion part of the parish. The Window Tax (1730) was collected in lower and higher divisions and reflects that the higher division was outstripping the lower in its overall wealth. It must have been irksome, therefore, for the inhabitants of the higher division to have their chapel served only once a month, and that by the minister of the lower division. Equally, one wonders, might that minister feel reluctance at that monthly visit to the *'dark and pagan place'* as Penclawdd was described at the time. Here was developing a divide between rural and industrial Wales. Even as late as the 19th century, however, we find legal transactions, such as those made for Starling Benson in acquiring properties around Penclawdd, making no distinction between the divisions of the parish - Penclawdd was consistently described as *'in Lanridian'*. This was in spite of the fact that all census returns and the tithe maps reflected the lower/higher division. It was not until 1924 that the church at Llanyrnewydd was officially incorporated into the 'parish' of Llanrhidian Higher. Today, the parish administration of both areas is carried out by the secular community councils of 'Llanrhidian Lower' and 'Llanrhidian Higher'.

The map on page 22 indicates some of the chief factors in dividing the parish in geographical terms.

Welsh Moor - probably so named because it represents the boundary between English and Welsh Gower.

Coal - from 1800

The difficulties experienced in the coal industry towards the end of the eighteenth century led to a considerable decline in output. Although new ventures were still being attempted, it seems that the capital needed for a revival of mining was not to hand. By 1808 the copper works, which were by then working in rather desultory fashion, received coal shipped from Llanelli on account of the local mines' failure to meet demand. An account of 1823 suggests that there was still no activity in local mines. In 1826, however, the Benson family began to acquire property in the area with a view to developing the potential for coal mining. Central to their acquisitions were the lands around the old Penlan farm which became the site of the Penclawdd Colliery. Capital investment was needed, however, and it was some 10 years before operations began in earnest. Benson also acquired the old metal works and was thus able to integrate both operations. The fortunes of this combined operation were a little erratic and it was not until the arrival of the railway in 1863 that coal mining really began to expand. This was particularly the case when the line reached Llanmorlais with vital sidings reaching up into the heart of the Morlais valley. By 1890 the entire length of the line from Berthlwyd to Llanmorlais was flanked by mine workings or sidings leading to mines.

Between 1880 and the First World War, coal mining was the key economic activity of the higher division of Llanrhidian. After the war there was both a national and local decline in the demand for coal and gradually the mines closed down. Three serious accidents in the area hastened the closure of pits - at the Brynlais Colliery (Llanmorlais) in 1924, at Killan Colliery in 1925 and at Wernbwll Colliery (Berthlwyd) in 1929. In a small community these three accidents, which between them claimed the lives of 16 men, were terrible blows. Within 5 years of the Wernbwll disaster there were only 2 pits (the 'Wern' and 'Gelli' at Llanmorlais) operating. The Second World War gave a little impetus to extract lower grade coal as at the Gelligroes colliery but by 1950 all mining activity had ceased. Although significant reserves still lie beneath the estuary, it seems unlikely that the economic conditions will ever return that will lead to another revival in local mining.

A North-South Section through Llanrhidian Coal Measures - showing the main veins worked

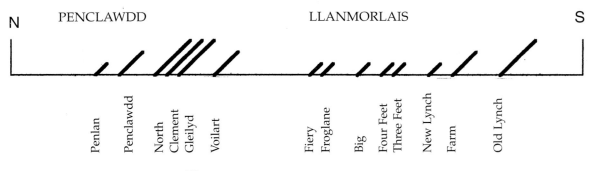

Mining was by no means a safe occupation – miners at the Lynch Collery at the beginning of this century could hear the waters over their heads! Flooding was a major problem, particularly if old workings were broken into. Gas was another frequent difficulty. Both of these hazards claimed lives– below is a list of fatal accidents that have occurred in the area.

A typical group of colliers from a Llanrhidian mine c1900

COLLIERY	DATE OF ACCIDENT	NO.OF FATALITEIS	CAUSE OF ACCIDENT
Wernffrwd	20th June 1795	4	Flooding due to breaking into old workings.
Penclawdd	19th Jan. 1844	1	Fell when descending pit.
Penclawdd	22nd April 1853	2	Explosion during blasting operation
Wernffrwd	5th June 1861	2	Flooding due to breaking into old workings. It was established that proper precautions had not been taken as old workings were approached.
Beaufort - Three Crosses	14th June 1867	3	Gas explosion
Brynlais	27th Oct. 1924	4	Explosion from gas in mine
Killan	27th Nov. 1924	5	Flooding from old workings - possibly due to inadequate precautions being taken
Wernbwll	28th Nov. 1929	7	Explosion from gas in mine

Collieries operating in Llanrhidian 1800 - 1950

Map No.	Colliery	Grid Ref.	Seams worked	Dates of operation and additional notes
1	Berthlwyd	561960	Hughes	1909-1931 operated with Wernbwll
2	Brynlais	539944	Froglane	1923-1924 - closed after explosion
3	Caer Eithin	561947		Part of Wernbwll/Berthlwyd
4	Cefn Bychan	544942	Penclawdd	1840-1850 flooded
5	Coed	534957	Big/New Lynch	part of Old Llanmorlais?
6	Crawfords	534943	Big/Froglane	1911-1918 problems with gas
7	Cwm Vale	541941		c1880
8	Dan y lan	554959		c1880
9	Dulas	532955	Clement	1909-1910 no coal found
10	Dwrllas	535958?	? Four Feet/Big	1930-1935 part of the Wern Coll.
11	Gelli	532951	Four Feet/Big	1885-1900 Coal lost in faulting
12	Gelligroes	533933	Farm	1939-1944 Poor quality coal
13	Gower Lynch	510940	Lynch	1920-1921 Closed in coal strike
14	Hinds	531944	Four Ft/Big/Froglane	c1924
15	Killan	582938		c1875-1925 closed after disastrous flood - also at 586941
16	Llanmorlais	534945	Big/Froglane	1820-1881 coal lost in faulting
17	Llanyrnewydd	547949	Voilart/Golden	1944-1950 mainly fireclay
18	Lower Llanmorlais	524945	Three & Four Feet/Big	
19	Lynch	522942	Lynch	1850-1855 worked out
20	Manchester	536958	Penlan	1890-1892 Poor quality coal
21	Morlais Vale	547939	Froglane/Big	1894 - gas problems
22	Old Llanmorlais	534944	Four Ft/Big	1880-85 & 1890-1900 flooded
23	Old Lynch	516939	Lynch	1909-1910
24	Old Penclawdd	543947	Penlan	1880-1882 Veins lost also at 554952
25	Old Penlan	532955?	Gleilyd/Clement	1989-1904 thin veins
26	Old Wernbwll	555952?	Clement	1893-1898 problems with faulting
27	Penclawdd	545956	Penclawdd/Clement	1847-1867 worked out
28	Penlan	533956		c1914
29	New Lynch	522944	New Lynch	1912-1916 extended under estuary /flooded
30	New Penlan	553959	Penclawdd	1908-1917 flooded
31	Tir Gill	538949	Gleilyd	1918-1920 prob. same as 'Gordon's Trigil'
32	Wern	534942	Four Ft/Big	1922-1935 flooded
33	Wern Bwll	554948	Penlan/Penclawdd	see 'Berthlwyd' - very extensive colliery - also at 561946
34	Western	532955	Clement/Penclawdd	1916-1925 - closed in depression
35	Whitewalls	560936	Big/Three Ft	1940-1948 - flooded

Note that 'Glammant' appears to have been interchangeable with 'Clement' in some accounts

Acknowledgement must be made to W G Davies's 'Coal in the Morlais Valley' - a dissertation submitted for a degree in 1956. A substantial part of this list relies on this important study which drew on much local information.

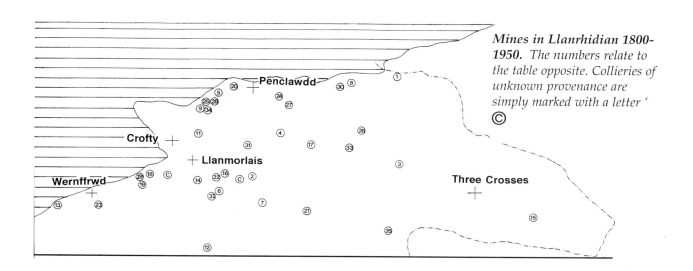

Penclawdd

Crofty

Llanmorlais

Wernffrwd

Three Crosses

This view of the industrial part of the village was taken about 1900. Prominent in the centre of the picture are the copper works and the tinplate works (a little to the left). On the right of the picture can be seen the tip of the Penclawdd Colliery and on the extreme left are two old thatched ro roof cottages - relics of the 18th century. It is worth noting how every spare bit of ground has been given over to food production, particularly potatoes.

Llanrhidian's Woollen Industry

The activities of George Dix at the Staffal-Haegr woollen mill are fairly well documented as part of Gower's heritage. The Staffal-Haegr mill was just a part of a weaving industry found across north-west Gower, with factories at Llanrhidian, Cheriton, Llangennith and near Sluxton. The origins of this industry are not clearly known but some detail can be 'painted-in' for the preceding centuries in Llanrhidian.

The Welsh woollen industry tended to develop in the late middle ages and through the 16th and 17th centuries as an unregulated, and consequently low quality, trade. J. Geraint Jenkins (The Welsh Woollen Industry 1969) described it as 'unorganised, widely scattered ....., incapable of self improvement'. In this context we have to take evidence of the wool trade in Llanrhidian during this early period at face value and not see it as part of a larger and more organised whole. For example, there is evidence of only paltry exports of processed wool from Swansea and it is likely that the town was a net importer of wool products. Local weavers, therefore, had an open market for their produce. In Llanrhidian, particularly in the west of the parish, there were large flocks of sheep to provide ample raw material for the industry. It is not surprising to find regular references in the wills of the parish to items connected with wool processing. In 1620 Jenkin Richard left a pair of looms and 14 pounds of wool; 9 years later Evan David also left a pair of looms. In 1638 Thomas David, described as 'weaver of Llanrhidian', gained a lease of Weobley Castle. When Evan Long died in 1667 he left his 'implements belonging to his trade' (of weaver). Hopkin Long, probably a close relative of Evan, left 'all the materials that belong to the trade of a weaver' to his son David in his will of 1685. There is also occasional reference to spinning wheels as in the will of Howell Thomas in 1674. Although there is a reference to a tucking mill on the Burry Stream in the time of Henry VIII (Penrice & Margam 3002) it is unlikely that there was much facility for quality finishing of cloth in the area and for this reason it is not surprising that the industry was unable to supply an export trade in spite of the abundance of wool.

This low-level, cottage-based, industry persisted through the 18th century. There is a specific reference to a weaver, George David, having land in the village with his garden adjoining the churchyard in 1744. Also, from 1749 we have the will of John Jenkin, a weaver of Llanrhidian. It can be seen, therefore, that when George Dix arrived early in the 19th century there was a long- standing tradition of wool manufacturing in the area. Dix was born in Neath but married a Llanrhidian girl. Brian Taylor (Gower 42) estimates that the mill at Staffal-Haegr began operation around 1820. It was fed by a leat running across the fields from the stream that fed the Llanrhidian higher and lower mills. It is likely that what was once a strong stream running from the hill under Penyrallt was the initial reason for locating the mill on that spot. George Dix's son, Joseph, took over the business and his grandson Richard was the last to work the looms there in 1904. The quilts and bedspreads of the Dix's factory were reputed to be of high quality.

The census of 1851 was taken when the Llanrhidian woollen industry was at its height. It reveals that although the main activity was focussed on Staffal Haegr there was also a great deal going on around the Lower Division of the parish. Even in the village of Crofty, next to Pencaerfenni Farm, weaving was going on at handlooms. It is likely that much of the production was coordinated by the Dix's although some may have had local outlets for their produce. The map below, based on the 1879 Ordnance Survey map, gives some idea of the extent of woollen manufacture around Llanrhidian in the mid 19th century. The ages given are those at the time of the 1851 census

STAFFAL HAEGR
George Dix 39
John Dix 19 Carder
George Dix 16 Spinner
Joseph Dix 15 Carder
Martin Dix 13 Quilt Maker
Thomas Dix 20 Weaver (George Dix's brother)

LLANRHIDIAN
John Tanner 60 Handloom weaver
John Phillip 56 Handloom weaver
Alford Batcock 17 Weaver's apprentice

WERNHALOG
19th century weaving activity according to H M Tucker (1951)

COMMON
Elizabeth Bevan 52 Spinner

OLDWALLS
David Jones 32 Handloom weaver
William Jones 13 Weaver's apprentice

WALTERSTON
Mary Tall 63 Spinner
Elizabeth William 27 Spinner

STONEYFORD
Thomas Gwyn 25 Handloom flannel weaver

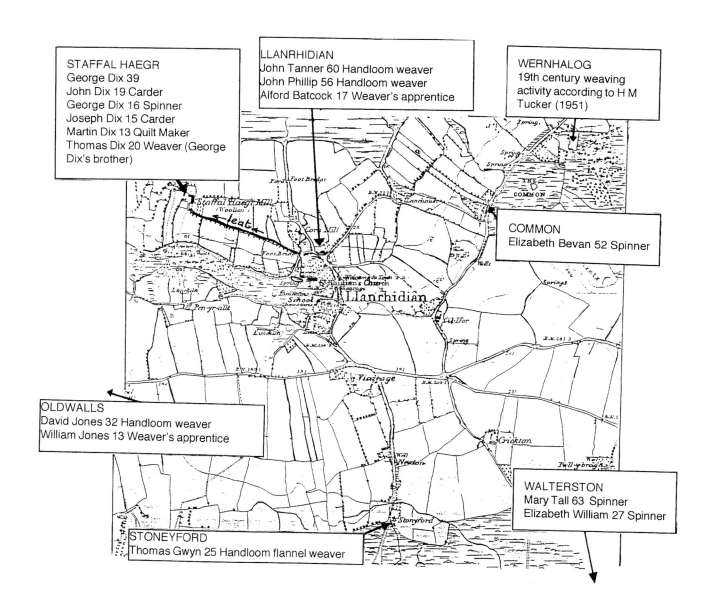

The Port of South Burry

1 Jacob Dumain

Jacob Dumain was appointed to the post of 'Waiter and Searcher at South Burry' on the 30th July 1721. It was a post he held until his death in 1730. Dumain was a man about whom we know nothing apart from the post he held and a few entries in the letter books of the Swansea Customs authority. But, in explaining who he was and what he did, we learn a great deal about the creeks and harbours of Llanrhidian's marshy coastline.

A limiting factor in the quantity of coal that could be exported was the fact that everything was brought to boats on horseback.

As 'waiter and searcher', Dumain was effectively in charge of an establishment for regulating the coal trade along the southern half of the Burry estuary from Pontardulais to Worm's Head. Penclawdd was the chief shipping place of this extensive port known collectively as the 'port of South Burry'. In the previous century the name 'Rhyd y lydan' (Broadford) was applied to these shipping places but, as far as the port of Swansea was concerned, 'South Burry' better defined the extent of the responsibilities held by Dumain. For example, at Cheriton was the 'tidesman and boatman' John Griffith; together with George Bydder and Richard Williams he was detailed to keep *'a watchful eye on the coast and observe all things coming into ye river of Burry'*. Any untoward happenings such as a small boat putting out from Weobley to meet an incoming vessel would have occasioned them to put out from Cheriton to see if contraband was being unloaded. Dumain had his own boat at Penclawdd and could use it to control smuggling but his main duties were supervising and measuring coal cargoes leaving the port. This was a most burdensome and contentious task requiring the presence of customs officers at loading places at Wernffrwd, Crofty, Penclawdd, Berthlwyd, Pont ar Cob (close to present day Gowerton) and Loughor. Not surprisingly, Dumain requested the use of a horse *'as his predecessor had'* in order to be able to keep an eye on this extensive port. A subsidiary 'room' was established at Loughor but Dumain must have had his hands full. Swansea customs noted in 1722 that he had *'abundance of business, the trade of that place (South Burry) being considerably advanced'*.

With a little imagination and some reference to surviving manuscripts we can picture Dumain at his work. For example, on the 29th January in 1727 he left his 'room' in Penclawdd to make a seizure on board the 'Mary'. His 'room' was, by tradition, close to today's 'Royal Oak' and the adjacent 'Beach Cottage' may well be substantially part of the 'room'. Vessels loading would, for the most part, be *'lyeing on the wast or strand'* about a hundred-or-so yards away. Most coal was being manhandled onto vessels for, as the letter book tells us in 1722, *'coals are not shipped here (in Penclawdd) in lighters, barges and carts as att Newcastle and Milford but in bags 48 whereof make a weigh'*. It was this lack of capital investment in the loading facilities that led to the decline of the port and coal industry in the latter part of the century. To make his seizure on board the 'Mary', Dumain would have been assisted by the officers at Penclawdd under his charge of which there were at least two. It would appear that there had been at least three officers in total for the previous forty or fifty years. He would also have been assisted by the fact that the port was not busy at the time; trade in winter was often quieter than in the summer. At the best of times, the passage up the estuary to Penclawdd was tortuous, in gales or against a stiff, icy, east wind access would have been well nigh impossible. Vessels could have been warped up the estuary on a rising tide. One vital factor in favour of the port, however, was that the course of the river was very close to the Penclawdd shore so that deep water was available at many states of the tide within a few yards of the foreshore in Penclawdd. In spite of this, by the middle of the century some vessels were refusing to run the risk of anchoring in the strong tides and insisted in the coal being brought to them in lighters at Whiteford. The Llanmorlais syndicate (p.68), operating between 1590 and 1630 had such lighters at their disposal.

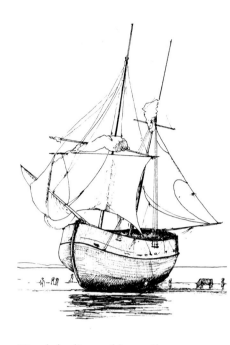

Vessels loading coal lay on the sands at low tide, as this copy of a painting by E Duncan (c1850) shows. The vessel is shown lying on the sands at Crofty.

As Dumain left his room he would probably have seen large piles of coal at various points by the road where mine owners and small colliers would deposit their produce ready for shipping. The Badminton papers record applications from a number of local colliers for permission to lay down 'coal banks' ready for shipping. The area on the foreshore and in front of cottages may well have looked an untidy but busy mess. Of the 'Mary' we know nothing except that it appeared to be a Penclawdd vessel. Most of these vessels were small by virtue of the constrictions on size made by the difficulties in the estuary. The main trade was in coastwise shipping of coal, principally to north Devon, Cornwall, southern Ireland and occasionally to France. There are no other records of seizures by Dumain in his 9 years as principle officer at the port and this seizure seemed to be very modest - a *'parcel of fresh provisions'*. This was probably a euphemism but, since a quantity was left on board sufficient for the ship's crew, we may assume that a substantial excess of 'fresh provisions' was on board. Perhaps Dumain was too busy most of the time to be searching ships' holds and ballast or rummaging in the warehouse but it is possible that he was a lenient officer, happy to turn a blind eye to 'fresh provisions' provided he had some share. Doubtless, also, there were occasions when he felt obliged to make a token seizure and, on the 29th January 1727, the 'Mary' was to be the victim.

It seems that life at Penclawdd was not ruffled by many untoward events. When Dumain was instructed, in 1728, to keep an eye on a square ended Loughor brigantine due to load coal for Holland some interest must have been injected into the work. This particular vessel was under the charge of Captain 'Hard Boy' Jones and was described as having *'a bad reputation and a lion carved in the head'*.

The letter books record, on the 2nd January 1730, that *'last night died Mr Jacob Dumain Waiter and coaster...'*. Three days later he was replaced by James Dalton who held the post for at least the next 38 years. In his first year in the job he had seized '2 *doz glass bottles of port wine .....lodyd in the warehouse'*, 3 casks each of 8 gallons of brandy and yet more brandy smuggled into Weobley. This activity may well be a

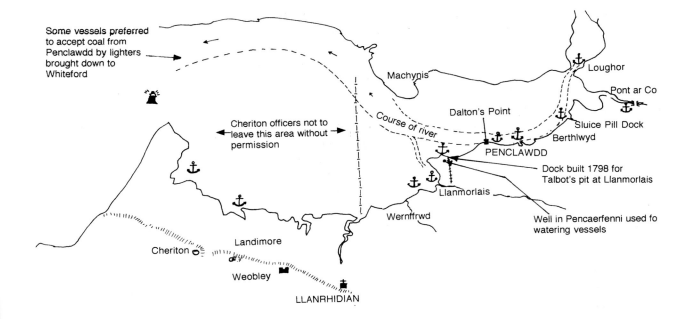

Labels in figure:
Some vessels preferred to accept coal from Penclawdd by lighters brought down to Whiteford

Machynis

Loughor

Pont ar Co

Course of river

Dalton's Point

Sluice Pill Dock

Cheriton officers not to leave this area without permission

Berthlwyd

PENCLAWDD

Dock built 1798 for Talbot's pit at Llanmorlais

Llanmorlais

Well in Pencaerfenni used fo watering vessels

Wernffrwd

Cheriton

Landimore

Weobley

LLANRHIDIAN

Llanrhidian - the chief shipping places.

commentary on the laxity of Jacob Dumain's days in the Penclawdd room but it is noticeable that after 1731 Dalton appears to have made no recorded seizures.

2. Thomas Prance

Thomas Prance remains Penclawdd's most illustrious son. In spite of this, his grave remains unmarked and his history unknown to many local people. The Prance family of Penclawdd was descended from the Prances of north Devon. Thomas's father, John, was from Appledore and married Mary German of Penclawdd in 1762. John's antecedents were all from Northam, a port close to Appledore. Interestingly, it was from Northam vessels that James Dalton confiscated 24 bottles of port wine and 24 gallons of brandy in 1730. Northam vessels were the most frequently recorded entries in the Penclawdd records at that time and it seems reasonable that it was through this agency that John came to the burgeoning village of Penclawdd. Mary German's father, John, was himself a mariner.

Thomas was born in 1768 and by the age of just 23 was captain of a vessel in the Mediterranean. A year later, in 1793, Prance was in the Atlantic - captain of the 'Joseph' and part of a convoy from Virginia to Spain. France had declared war on Britain on the 1st February and it was a French vessel, the 'Sans Culotte' (10 guns), that caught the 'Joseph' (2 guns) trailing at the back of the convoy. An engagement of arms ensued over the next 3 days. The battle concluded with Prance, already injured in the leg, forced to surrender on account of losing both his hands which had been blown off by a prematurely exploding charge in a cannon. It had been a long and courageous fight and Prance was so badly wounded that he was assumed dead in Britain. Surviving, however, his reappearance in his home country was greeted as something of a sensation. With the approbation of the Prince Regent he received 1000 guineas.

With the massive handicap of losing both hands, one might have expected Prance to retire to a life of modest comfort but he was too active for this. With the aid of frames and attachments to his elbows and arms he was able to steer boats, to board vessels, to inspect holds, even to use to a knife and fork and to write. His vessel 'Endeavour' was fitted out for service with the Royal Navy in convoying vessels in the Bristol Channel. In 1802 he married Martha Williams in Penclawdd and subsequently had 6 children. In July 1807 he became the 'sitter' in the Whiteford boat and 4 years later sold his vessel 'Endeavour' at Penclawdd. In the execution of his duties for the customs service he showed something close to an excess of vigour. Resurrecting the old 'Sea-fencibles', a local militia originally organised as a sort of 'home guard' in the French Wars, he confiscated significant amounts of contraband that he found at Rhossili in his first year in the service. In February, 1811, we find him involved in raising the sloop 'Elizabeth' at Whiteford. To what extent his Swansea counterparts welcomed his enthusiasm is open to question and for the next few years we hear nothing of Prance.

In the year 1815, however, he re-enters the records. The following account is in Prance's own words and it should be noted that other submissions made to the Customs Office painted a different picture - putting considerable blame on Prance. It should be pointed out, as well, that the port at Penclawdd was very quiet during these years with an almost complete cessation in copper and coal cargoes leaving and entering. It would appear that a number of the Penclawdd officers were 'off-station' (they should have been at Whiteford or Cheriton) with the consequence that the arrival of a French vessel in the estuary was, initially, unnoticed on the Penclawdd side.

'Penclawdd Decr. 3rd 1815

Gentlemen
Your letter of this day I this moment received: in reply to which I beg leave to notice that at half past 12 p.m. fresh gales and very hazy weather, I received information by express of the vessel you mention of and immediately despatched one of the boatmen William Thomas to Llanmadock and Whitford to watch and attend thereon, whilst I proceeded with the boat. Evan Francis and four glutmen (William Webb and Joseph Davies being at Customs to receive the pay for the month) early on the flood against adverse winds and tide to meet said vessel, on the passage down the river we discover'd on shore near Machynis having drifted up the previous flood with a number of boats alongside and men employed warping her off for the port of Llanelly, at 4 p.m. called alongside and found her to be a French Brig ('Concorde') laden with brandy and wine from some port in France dismasted and a perfect wreck; not observing a proper officer left on board by the Customs at Llanelly only glutmen and a few extramen to protect so valuable a cargo. I put Evan Francis on board to remain there until my return after taking some refreshment etc. when the vessel was dry I came alongside again, when I observed much noise and altercation

amongst the men on board and was informed that during my absence one of the Llanelli officers had fell overboard and was drowned and the one I had left on board in the ship Evan Francis incapable of duty from a state of intoxication and in an hour after or thereabouts I was the first person that discovered the vessel to be on fire in the forecastle and from her being dry and no water near her, it increased in opposition to every effort to extinguish it, until put out by the flood tide after having destroyed the greater part of the cargo in the twindecks and very materially injur'd the hull.

When Mr Nevil (who see'd to have taken on him the management of the ship and cargo) came on board early in this morning and was informed by the Llanelly men that I had left an officer on board and the fault rested with my officers and boats crew, he gave me very insolent language threatening that if he had been there he would throw us overboard, that I had no business there and wonder'd the Llanelli glutman Lloyd had not cut us down threatening also to report me and crew. At 6 a.m. when the port surveyor came on board I asked him if there was any occasion for my further services - he said no, and seemed much displeased I should have been on that serivce.

I have nothing to say in extenuation of Evan Francis's conduct having acted so palpably wrong only his being a very young officer and it is the first offence of the kind

I am etc

Thos. Prance Sitter

The extent to which the Llanelli customs men thought that the Penclawdd officers were interfering with, or 'cashing in on', the prize wreck of the 'Concorde' can be guessed at through Prance's own account. In their own depositions it was clear that there had been anything but concord in the middle of the estuary and that Prance was held largely to blame for the events. With hindsight it can be seen that the Llanelli men were, possibly, quite out of order before the Penclawdd boat arrived, whose arrival merely compounded the problems. Prance received a severe reprimand for his part in affairs, Evan Francis lost his job as a result of his *'riotous and disorderly conduct'*, all the other Penclawdd men involved were never to be employed by the customs again.

A strange postscript to the story of Thomas Prance relates to the mystery of his unmarked grave. He died in 1837 and was buried in Penclawdd in the Llanyrnewydd churchyard. For such an illustrious man to have no surviving headstone seemed strange until an explanation was given to this writer a few years ago. The church was altered in 1926 and in the course of work one of the men engaged, who later gave this account, had to remove the floor from the west end of the church. Beneath the floor he found a skeleton that puzzled him, it was a skeleton without hands. The bones were removed and buried in an unmarked spot outside. If this was the burial of Thomas Prance, as seems highly likely, the explanation remains difficult, for why was the original burial not marked by a slab above it on the floor of the chapel? This can be explained by the fact that the chapel-of-ease in which he was originally buried (being a distinguished son of the village it is not surprising that he was buried inside the building) was dismantled and rebuilt in 1851. It was probably decided that Prance's burial should be kept within the building at that time since he was still well-remembered but, not surprisingly, the burial slab was lost in the rebuilding.

3. Howell John

Howell John and William Howell of Llanmadoc were partners in seafaring business. At Penclawdd, Howell John established a shipyard which, for a short period, must have ranked as one of the more important in south Wales. There had been a long tradition of shipbuilding skills in the area (witness the will of John Long, shipwright, in 1690) and tradition has it that the oaks of Pencaerfenni were used in Nelson's navy. Just prior to Howell John there appears to have been some shipbuilding in the village. John Bennet (probably of Cwm Cynnar) rebuilt the 'Lark', a 29 foot sloop from Oxwich in 1828, the year before Howell John began operations.

The shipyard was right on Dalton's Point, immediately to the west of the 'Pink Cottages'. During its last 10 years of operation it must have added excitingly to the skyline of the village.

The site of the shipbuilding yard of Howell John as it appears today in the 'West End' of the village.

Vessels built in Penclawdd between 1826 and 1840

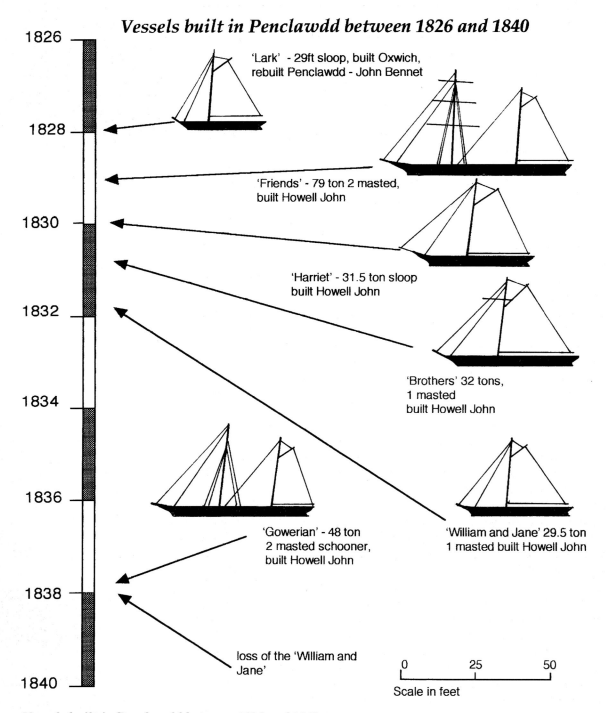

1826
1828
1830
1832
1834
1836
1838
1840

'Lark' - 29ft sloop, built Oxwich,
rebuilt Penclawdd - John Bennet

'Friends' - 79 ton 2 masted,
built Howell John

'Harriet' - 31.5 ton sloop
built Howell John

'Brothers' 32 tons,
1 masted
built Howell John

'Gowerian' - 48 ton
2 masted schooner,
built Howell John

'William and Jane' 29.5 ton
1 masted built Howell John

loss of the 'William and
Jane'

0   25   50
Scale in feet

Vessels built in Penclawdd between 1826 and 1840
Source - Swansea Shipping Register D/DPRO/RBS/5 132 held in the Swansea Archives Office.

The Way to Llanrhidian

One of the fascinations of history in a locality is that every little detail of the landscape may have a meaning or nuance in the context of the story of the area. We may find that an overgrown footpath or even an old hedgerow is all that remains of an ancient way. In both the lower and higher parts of our parish the ancient ways have, to some extent been superseded by a 'modern' road, built between the two world wars, joining the settlements strung out along the coast of north Gower. Before this road was built travel was very different in the area. Until this century a great deal of the network of roads in Gower served to feed the traffic to and from Swansea. Like the roots of a great tree drawing the nutrients of trade and produce from the remotest parts and feeding them to Swansea, trackways spread out along the ridges (always the driest line for a trackway) west of the town. Like 'rootlets', lanes dropped from the ridges, dividing and subdividing in order to reach each little hamlet or farmstead.

The Swansea-Llanrhidian Coach Service before motorisation.

The main way to Llanrhidian followed the ridgeway from Dunvant to Three Crosses. At that point traffic could fork onto the ridge north of the Morlais valley to Cefn Bychan or it could follow the ridge on the south side of the valley, climbing past Cilonnen and on to Welsh Moor before dropping to Llanrhidian itself. This latter route may only have been superseded in the turnpike age (after 1764) by the road cutting across Fairwood and Pengwern Commons to Cilibion. From the old trackways, unimpeded at first by fields and enclosures, 'feeder lanes' dropped down to Penclawdd, Crofty, Cwm Cynnar, Wernffrwd and Wernhalog. Because of the Swansea orientation it was difficult to move from one settlement to another without getting up onto the main ridgeway. True, there was a way along the edge of the marsh but that, frequently inundated by tides and probably nearly unusable for wheeled traffic, was of very limited use.

The Turnpike Act of 1764 made provision for two roads in Gower one of which was to serve the burgeoning village of Penclawdd. Unfortunately, we know little of the details of this road except that it ran from Three Crosses where, near the poundfold, there was a turnpike gate (site of a Rebecca Riot in 1843), down to Penclawdd reaching the waterside by the old Ship and Castle Inn. To some extent this would have been improving an old ridgeway track made tortuous by progressive enclosures. It is likely that new stretches of road were constructed at the Penclawdd end from Penyrheol to the site of the Blue Anchor Inn and from Caban Isaac across the hillside to Banc Bach. This last construction can be inferred from the knowledge that a century before there appears to have been no such way in existence at that point. A survey of Knelston manor, made in 1688, of lands which were to become part of the Dunraven estate mentions nothing more than an old ditch in the vicinity.

Similar improvements on roads near Cilibion may have led to the abandonment of what is clearly an ancient way that climbs the ridge from Llethrid towards Prysg Farm by Welshmoor. A document of the 15th century (see appendix 2) suggests that this was an ancient way from Llethrid to Wernhalog and even during the last century was known as 'Black Lane'. Today it is no more than an overgrown footpath wending its way through some of the loveliest bluebell woods in Gower.

In 1871 David Thomas advertised (in the 'Cambrian') his carrying service from Swansea to Penclawdd. Starting at the Oxford Inn in Swansea it ran on Wednesdays and Saturdays at 5 pm. He was hardly able to compete with the railways' developing services especially since he had to follow such a difficult route on poor roads. It was not until 1931 that the new 'tarmacadamed' road from Gowerton to Llanrhidian was completed. It is difficult to imagine the transformation this made as we drive along its gentle curves. In 1800 a coal cart might have taken half a day travelling to Llanrhidian from Llanmorlais and back, today the same return journey could be accomplished in under 10 minutes. The 'New Road', as it is still known in Crofty, is one of the most significant changes of the last 400 years.

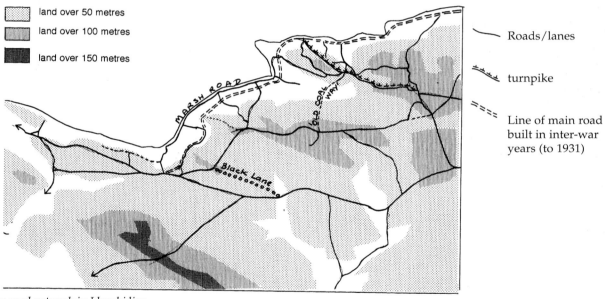

land over 50 metres
land over 100 metres
land over 150 metres

Roads/lanes

turnpike

Line of main road built in inter-war years (to 1931)

The road network in Llanrhidian c1800

1764 Turnpike Tolls - Gower
Draught animals with passenger vehicles - 3d
Draught animals with vehicles of lime and manure - 2d
Unladen draught animals -1d
Droves of cattle or oxen - 10d a score
Calves, sheep, lambs or swine - 5d a score

Starling Benson

Starling Benson was an important influence in the history of Penclawdd. His memory is still recalled in the village in such names as 'Benson Street' and 'Benson Terrace'. Significant areas of the village are still held by the Benson Estate. In the early decades of the nineteenth century the economic condition of Penclawdd was very depressed. The coal mines, for want of investment, good seams and adequate transport, were barely in existence and unable to supply the needs of industry. The copper works, thriving at the turn of the century, were closed. The failure of the mines was probably a major factor in the closure. All around the village were the signs of blighted activity - grassy spoil heaps, smokeless chimneys, overgrown railroads and shipless quays. The arrival of Starling Benson was to change much of this and presaged the period of Penclawdd's greatest importance.

Starling was born in what is now Greater London, the son of Thomas Starling Benson of North Cray Place in Kent and nearby Sanderstead Court in Surrey. Thomas inherited a plot of land in Swansea and came to the town in 1831 to see what good use could be made of it. He became involved in projects to 'float' the North Dock - involving his own land. The financial ramifications led to acrimony between Benson and the town's leading 'lights'. But Starling was making his own way in the world and on his own merits, sufficiently to become a trustee of the Swansea Harbour Trust (1836), Mayor of Swansea (1843) and chairman of the Harbour Trust (1856 to 1878). Called by John Dillwyn Llewelyn *'old Shylock'*, he was known to many as *'spare topmast'* on account of his great height. Whatever friends or enemies felt about him he was clearly a man of intellect and great energy. He had an enduring passion for geology and palaeantology which he indulged with his friend W E Logan around the cliffs and caves of Gower. Exhibits that are the result of his work can still be seen in the museum of the Royal Institution of South Wales (of which Starling was a most active member).

From about 1826, the Bensons had begun to acquire leases of land around Penclawdd - especially the area of the old copper works and the neighbouring coal mines. With William Logan he set up a copper company in 1834. A new pit was sunk at the Penclawdd Colliery and, in the early 1840's, they re-opened the metal works. There was sound business in this enterprise but there was philanthropy too. The local school at Banc Bach, the first of its kind in the village, was a foundation of Starling Benson's. During this period, Benson and Logan were faced with considerable financial difficulties from 1839 until the partnership was dissolved in 1850. Benson maintained his interest in the Penclawdd ventures throughout these difficulties but had to let go of the copper works in 1847 (they were taken over by Christopher Low). In 1858, at the age of 50, Starling Benson moved to 'Fairyhill' in West Gower and appears to have begun ridding himself of some of his business responsibilities. He maintained his interest in the Penclawdd estates and in personal transactions with villagers right up to his death in 1879. This

Starling Benson.
Photo courtesy of
Col. J. R. E. Benson.
Photograph originally published in
"From Fox How to Fairy Hill" by
J. N. Harding.

occurred when he was out shooting with his nephew, Richard Erle Benson. He appeared to have lost his footing on the edge of a quarry, slipped and fallen. He injured his head so badly that he died within the day.

This account relies heavily on the meticulous study, 'Starling Benson of Swansea', by Dorothy Bayliss and Joan Harding (pub. 1996 David Brown). This work gives extremely detailed accounts of Starling Benson's dealings in connection with his Penclawdd estates.

Waunarlwydd's Lost Route to the Sea.

When mining began around Waunarlwydd at the beginning of the 19th century it seemed to the mine owners (Messrs. Lockwood, Morris and Leyson) that the most effective way of getting their coals to market was via a canal leading down to Penclawdd where access would be gained to a seaway. Construction of this 4 mile long canal was begun in 1811 and within 2 years coals were ready for export at the 'new dock' which had to be constructed at Abercedi for this purpose. After a very few years of desultory use the canal became disused and was subsequently built over for much of its length by the railway. Very little is left of the canal but enough remains to indicate that the waterway was a standard 8 feet wide. Remains can be seen around Gowerton where a lock gate was converted to an air raid shelter. The bed of the canal can be seen where it was not built over by the railway as at Berthlwyd; here the course curved sharply round a marsh 'bay' which the railway later cut straight across. Also near Gowerton a part of the towpath is still a public footpath. The most interesting survival is, however, the dock terminal at Penclawdd which survives as a distinct promontory pointing out into the marsh. The scouring reservoir clearly survives beside it as does the site of the sluice which released the waters into the bed of the dock. This was a standard method around the Burry inlet for combatting silting of the dock.

The route of the Penclawdd Canal from Waunarlwydd to Penclawdd.

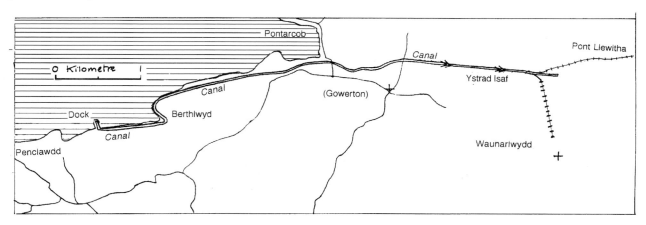

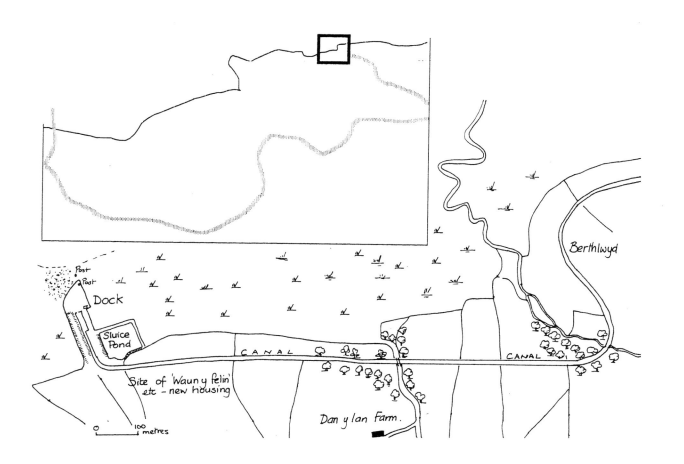

Above - the route of the Penclawdd Canal within the parish
Below - reconstruction of the canal dock as it would have appeared in 1812. The quay (1) and sluice pond (1) are to the right. There may have been a 'draw' bridge between 3 and 4 - this would have made the necessary provision of access to the nearby village of Penclawdd.

The Railway

With roads wholly inadequate to the transport of coal and a seaway becoming increasingly difficult to navigate, the survival of Penclawdd depended on some new lifeline. During the 1850's the coal towns of south Wales began to link up with the new railway from England which progressively reached Swansea, Llanelli and beyond. Brunel's viaduct at Loughor was built in full view of Penclawdd in 1852 and it must have occurred to anxious villagers that this was to be the way of survival for them. But it was not until 1861 that the line to Penclawdd was authorised under an enactment for the Llanelly Railway and Dock Company and it was another 6 years before the branch was opened.

The branch from Gower Road (Gowerton) to Penclawdd was three miles long and, being built largely along the line of the old canal, required no great engineering feats. At first there were no passenger services because the line was not built for that purpose. Along its length, sidings ran into a number of collieries and coal was the main freight throughout most of the life of the branch. In 1868, however, a passenger service was introduced running on just Wednesdays and Saturdays - within 15 years there was a minimum of four passenger trains a day (except on Sundays).

In 1873 the London and North Western Railway took over the branch which was subsequently extended another two miles to Llanmorlais. The extended branch began operations in 1877 (goods only) with a passenger service beginning on St David's Day, 1884. From the Llanmorlais terminus, sidings and tramways effectively extended the line right up into the Morlais valley enabling collieries to operate in immediate contact with the railway.

At its height the railway was really busy with coal traffic with at least a dozen sidings feeding as many coal mines all along its length. In addition there were the passenger services that ran trains with as many as seven coaches on Saturday mornings (too big to fit properly into Penclawdd station). Such trains would have been enlivened with the presence (and smell) of the cockle trade and were laden with the fruits of cockle sales in the Saturday return trains. Bolts of cloth were hurled from the windows as the train passed Berthlwyd - the passengers would be able to walk back to their homes there, unencumbered by the load. This train on a Saturday afternoon, eagerly awaited by the rest of the family, became known as the 'Relish Train'.

The decline of the railway coincided both with the decline of the coal mines and the building of the new road from Gowerton to Llanrhidian (1922 to 1928). Faced with the depressed state of the national economy and competition from buses, the London Midland and Scottish Railway, who had acquired the line in 1923, withdrew passenger services early in 1931. The Royal Ordnance factory at Crofty enabled some goods services to continue through the war but the last daily freight train ran on the 2nd September 1957. The track was lifted two years later.

(I am indebted to Mr Nigel Wassell for much information here - he is undoubtedly the foremost authority on this subject.)

Penclawdd railway station, 1873. At this date, Penclawdd was still the terminus of the branch line which was then part of the Swansea and Carmarthen Railways Co.. The locomotive is a Ramsbottom DX Goods 0-6-0. Behind the tree on the left are, just visible, some trams standing on the tramway of the Penclawdd Colliery. The white building to the right of the train was the Oddfellows Arms, demolished to make way for the extension to Llanmorlais and re-erected as the 'New Oddfellows Arms', now the "Railway Inn".
Thanks to Mr N Wassell for information pertaining to this photograph.
Photograph from the Stephen Rowson Collection, by kind permission.

The same place, 39 years later (1912), notice the cockles in baskets held on heads in the background

The same view, 1998

Farms and Homesteads

There are few, if any, remains of the old farms from which the settlement of the parish developed. In some cases new farms have been built on old foundations (as at Cefn Bychan) but, in many, all traces of the original settlement have vanished. In odd corners of the parish, however, intriguing ruins are to be found - usually just foundations as at the site of the old Tir Coch farm or the Lodge Farm near Cillibion. In some cases there are substantial survivals of buildings from the 17th or 18th century. Here is just a selection. (Ordnance Survey references in brackets)

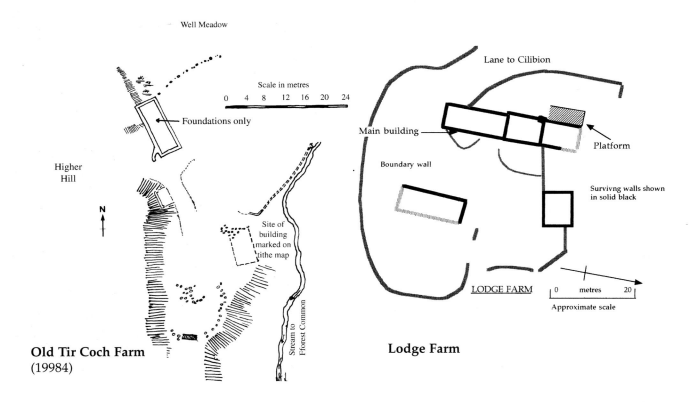

Old Tir Coch Farm
(19984)

Lodge Farm

Two Llanrhidian Farms

Old Tir Coch Farm (532929) was possibly a late Tudor farmstead nestling in a fold of the moors around the headwaters of the Llethrid stream. It was abandoned in the 19th century. An informal arrangement of buildings must have developed around a favoured spot. The main farmhouse (12m x 5m) was probably thatched and had one basic room at ground level (probably partitioned) with additional space in the attic.
Lodge Farm (521908) Originally associated with the hunting of Parc le Breos in medieval days, the remains of this farm date from the post Tudor period. Like Tir Coch, it was abandoned in the 19th century. It shows a similar, informal, arrangement of buildings. The site, in a gentle fold of the land sloping down from Cefn Bryn, close to runnng water, is also similar. It is hard to believe how Will Davies, the farmer in 1850, managed to live in such a confined area as the main farm house (19m x 5m) with his wife and 7 children.

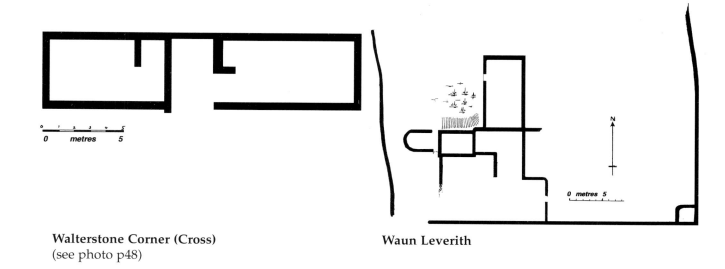

Walterstone Corner (Cross)
(see photo p48)

Waun Leverith

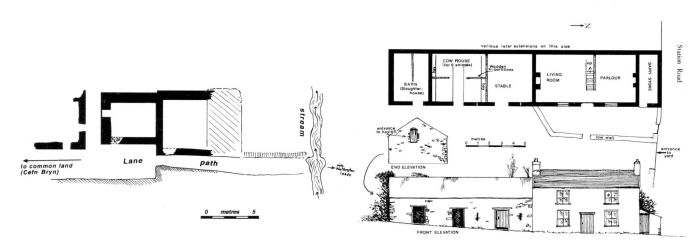

'Walter Tucker's House'

Llanmorlais Farm

Walterstone has a number of 'lost' farms and settlements including the well known lost village of Walterstone (qv). Nearby is the ruin of a 'long-house', abandoned last century and known as **Walterstone Corner (507898)**. Nearby is **'Walter Tucker's House'(511904)**, a cottage in which Walter and his wife, Mary, lived with their daughter Mary in 1851 (census). Close to the edge of the common, Walter was doubtless able to keep geese, a few cows and some pigs to add to his income as a gardener. **Waun Leverith(513904)**, a complete ruin, is something of a mystery. The remains are clearly of a well-established farm but there is no record of such a place as a habitation. It is mentioned in a survey of 1648 at which time it must have been inhabited but there is no direct evidence of this. Neither does it fit the 'long house tradition' typical of much of the parish - it may relate to some post-medieval settlement of the Walterstone estate.

The 'long -house' type farm building is well represented in the parish, particularly in the more Welsh higher division. **Llanmorlais Farm** (533946)- probably dating from from the 17th century, the present buildings are of 17th-18th century date.

Farms and Homesteads - Cefn Bychan

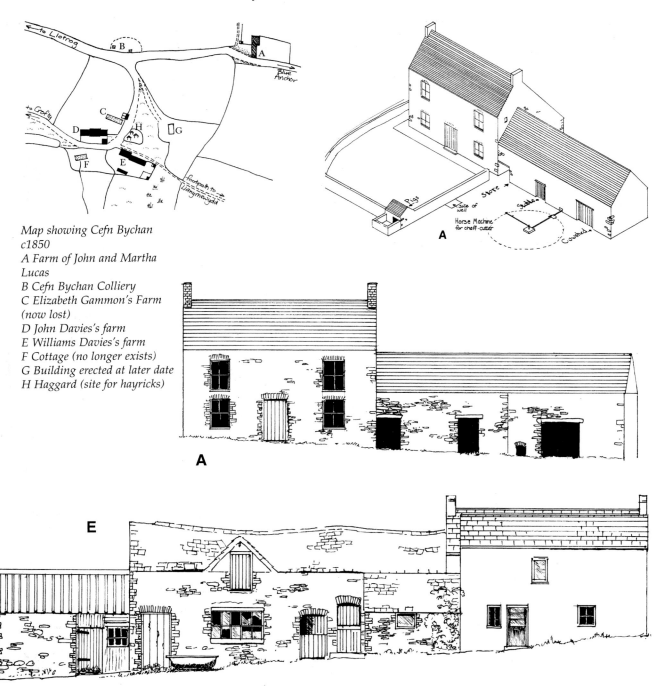

Map showing Cefn Bychan
c1850
A Farm of John and Martha
Lucas
B Cefn Bychan Colliery
C Elizabeth Gammon's Farm
(now lost)
D John Davies's farm
E Williams Davies's farm
F Cottage (no longer exists)
G Building erected at later date
H Haggard (site for hayricks)

One of the oldest and most representative groups of local vernacular buildings is to be found at
Cefnbychan (544951). Of the farms standing in the mid-nineteenth century, John and Martha Lucas's (A)
and Will Davies's (E) still have significant survivals.

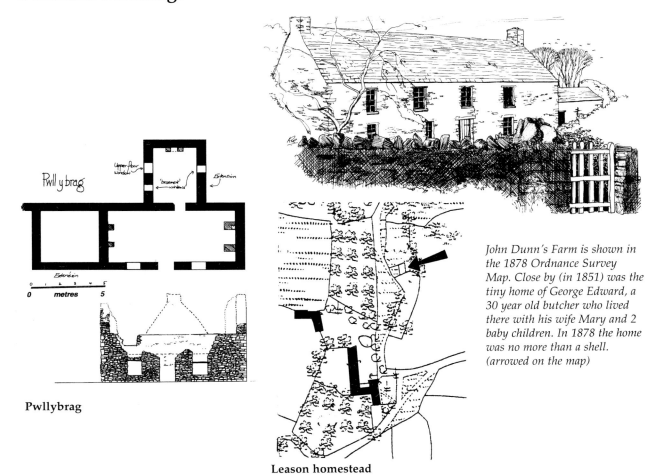

Pwll y brag

Pwllybrag

Leason homestead

John Dunn's Farm is shown in the 1878 Ordnance Survey Map. Close by (in 1851) was the tiny home of George Edward, a 30 year old butcher who lived there with his wife Mary and 2 baby children. In 1878 the home was no more than a shell. (arrowed on the map)

Although not a wealthy parish, it can be seen that Llanrhidian accommodated a wide range of inhabitants from the poorest classes up to the more affluent middle classes. Very little remains of the homes of the poorest people prior to the 19th century apart from the foundations of a few old cottages, usually about 6 metres by 3 metres. They can be seen at road sides where a little encroachment was achieved, examples are near Gelligroes Farm (535935), Tircoch (538930) and Leason (483926). In the lower division a typical small yeoman's house is well represented by **Pwllybrag** (506916). Dated by the RCAHM as c1800 this may be older - it is mentioned frequently in the leet court proceedingsas the home of Philip Jenkins in the early 18th century and cited as being in poor repair. In 1851 it was the home of William Lloyd, a carpenter and painter, and his wife Caroline who was a straw bonnet maker from Swaffham in Norfolk. **Leason Homestead** (482925) is a larger home-cum-farm of a relatively wealthy landowner. It probably dates from the middle of the 18th century, a period when many houses of this size were built in the area. In 1851 it was the home of John Dunn, farmer of 70 acres. He lived there together with his 7 children aged 2 to 17, his 80 year old mother and 4 servants. In stark contrast, just opposite the Leason Homestead are the remains of the tiny cottage which, in 1851, belonged to George Edwards. He was a butcher and lived there with his wife Ann and their two little children Philip (2) and Mary (3 months).

The Barracks - Penclawdd

Built as part of the original copperworks complex, this terrace has long been demolished. Thanks to photographs and the census we can recall both the buildings and their inhabitants as they were in 1881.

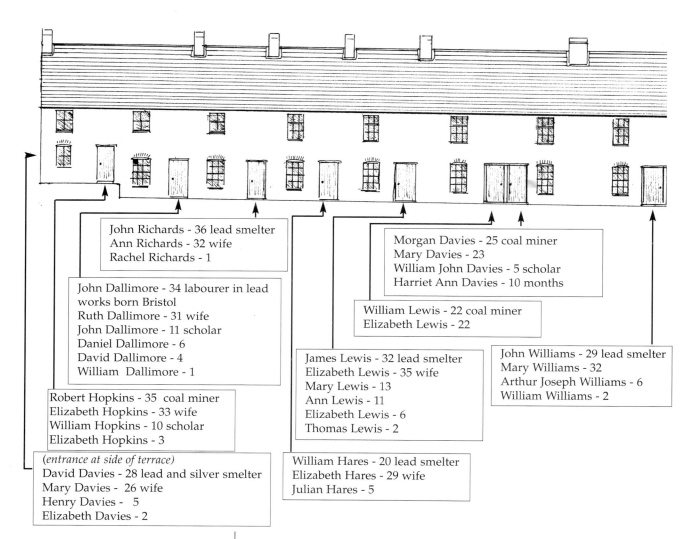

John Richards - 36 lead smelter
Ann Richards - 32 wife
Rachel Richards - 1

John Dallimore - 34 labourer in lead
works born Bristol
Ruth Dallimore - 31 wife
John Dallimore - 11 scholar
Daniel Dallimore - 6
David Dallimore - 4
William Dallimore - 1

Robert Hopkins - 35 coal miner
Elizabeth Hopkins - 33 wife
William Hopkins - 10 scholar
Elizabeth Hopkins - 3

(entrance at side of terrace)
David Davies - 28 lead and silver smelter
Mary Davies - 26 wife
Henry Davies - 5
Elizabeth Davies - 2

Morgan Davies - 25 coal miner
Mary Davies - 23
William John Davies - 5 scholar
Harriet Ann Davies - 10 months

William Lewis - 22 coal miner
Elizabeth Lewis - 22

James Lewis - 32 lead smelter
Elizabeth Lewis - 35 wife
Mary Lewis - 13
Ann Lewis - 11
Elizabeth Lewis - 6
Thomas Lewis - 2

William Hares - 20 lead smelter
Elizabeth Hares - 29 wife
Julian Hares - 5

John Williams - 29 lead smelter
Mary Williams - 32
Arthur Joseph Williams - 6
William Williams - 2

Station Row - this well known terrace was being built at the time of the 1881 census and would have (probably) been an object of interest and envy to the inhabitants of the 'Barracks' across the railway line.

The individual houses of Barracks Row offered accomodation well above the level of a typical agricultural labourer's home in the rural parts of the parish. Compared with the crude cottages around Walterstone they were better built and, considering they had an upper floor which was lacking in the smaller country cottages, were nearly twice as large in the floor area they offered. Even so, the floor area available in individual homes in Station Row (bottom of opposite page) was nearly twice as great again as that in Barracks Row. Although relatively small, Barracks Row is remembered in the village as having contained neat, pleasant homes with red brick floors.

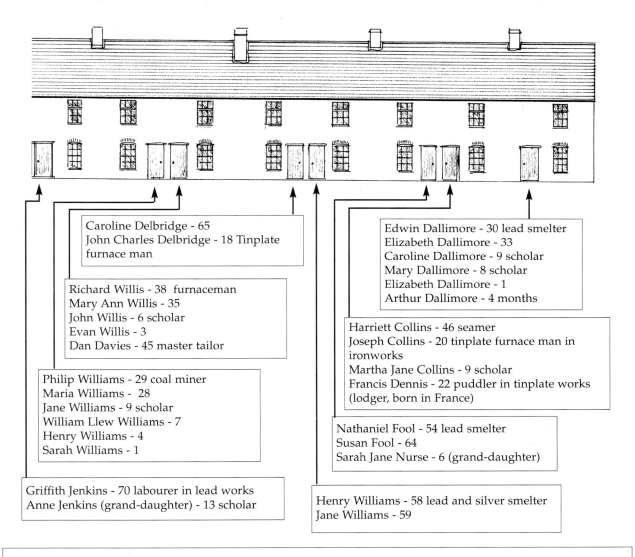

Caroline Delbridge - 65
John Charles Delbridge - 18 Tinplate
furnace man

Richard Willis - 38 furnaceman
Mary Ann Willis - 35
John Willis - 6 scholar
Evan Willis - 3
Dan Davies - 45 master tailor

Philip Williams - 29 coal miner
Maria Williams - 28
Jane Williams - 9 scholar
William Llew Williams - 7
Henry Williams - 4
Sarah Williams - 1

Griffith Jenkins - 70 labourer in lead works
Anne Jenkins (grand-daughter) - 13 scholar

Edwin Dallimore - 30 lead smelter
Elizabeth Dallimore - 33
Caroline Dallimore - 9 scholar
Mary Dallimore - 8 scholar
Elizabeth Dallimore - 1
Arthur Dallimore - 4 months

Harriett Collins - 46 seamer
Joseph Collins - 20 tinplate furnace man in
ironworks
Martha Jane Collins - 9 scholar
Francis Dennis - 22 puddler in tinplate works
(lodger, born in France)

Nathaniel Fool - 54 lead smelter
Susan Fool - 64
Sarah Jane Nurse - 6 (grand-daughter)

Henry Williams - 58 lead and silver smelter
Jane Williams - 59

Barracks Row was fairly representative of Penclawdd's working population in 1881, particularly of the 'new' part of the village around the railway station. The majority of these people were native to the parish or north Gower but the Dallimores (both families) and the Hares came from Bristol, the Fools from Frome in Somerset, the Delbridges from St Austell in Cornwall, William Lewis's wife Elizabeth was from Gwennap in Cornwall and Richard Willis's wife Mary was from Exeter. In addition, Dan Davies was from Narberth in Pembrokeshire whilst Griffith Jenkins, John Richards and John Williams came from across the estuary

Two Llanrhidian Farms————————————

1. Penrallt

Standing at the top of the old wooded cliffs that descend so steeply to the great spread of the marsh, Penrallt ('top of the wooded bank') is aptly named. It is first mentioned in a document of 1472, the year after Bosworth, and probably grew from the consolidation of Llanrhidian's common fields in the period after the Black Death and Glyndwr's rebellion. The manuscript of 1472 describes Hoskin Thomas receiving the 'messuage of Penralthe' and it may be that 'Hoskin's Close' and 'Hoskin's Park' (see map) are names that survive from the earliest period of the farm. These would have been enclosures from the common field of the village people and it is quite likely that Hoskin's farm was in the village itself on the site of what was to become known as 'Eastern Penrallt'. The process of enclosure and consolidation was still going on in the 1700's when we find the Prichard family engaged in dispute with the leet court about access for the villagers to their fields - this would have been hindered by taking selected strips into private ownership.

By 1600 the farm had already been split in two parts - in 1601 it was shared between the Prichards and Robert Harry, by 1665 the Prichard's had both tenements. In 1756, when the farm was divided between John Lucas and Evan Long, we learn that the two farms held respective seats in the church - a carefully awarded privilege. Eastern Penrallt, possibly the senior of the two, held a seat on the south side of 'the alley' whilst the other portion held a seat on the north side. Robert Prichard, whose gravestone hangs on the outside of the church wall, sat on the south side of the alley. His is just one of a number of wills that survive from the 17th and 18th centuries and give us a detailed picture of the farm.

Through wills dating from 1606 to 1717 we can see that Penrallt was essentially a mixed farm, rather stronger on sheep (flocks up to 50) than on dairy stock (herds up to 6). Arable was important, in a small way, but the keeping of store cattle only seems significant in wills around 1697. At that time it would appear that pigs were a major investment - possibly 20 were kept - they may have grubbed in the woods.

Even in the 18th century, the Prichards appeared to have holdings in surviving common fields. Gradually the farm extended into the lands south of the highway from Swansea to Llangennith, a process probably completed in the 18th century.

Penrallt Farm, seen from the main road.

104

Penrallt Cottage, the oldest surviving building and, for some time, the farmhouse of the eastern part of the farm.

The gravestone of Robert Prichard, farmer of Penrallt, who died in 1717. The stone is affixed to the south wall of the church. The inventory of his will reads:

Purse, watch, wearing apparel	£10
2 cows	£3
30 sheep	£3
1 heifer	£
2 calves	10s
1 pig	2s
10 lambs	5s
2 feather beds etc	£5
3 dust beds, linen etc	£1
Brass and pewter	£1
3 bedsteads	10s
2 chairs, a round table	5s
1 long table, 2 chests of drawers	£1
Silver salt cellar, a looking glass	10s
Implements of husbandry	2s 6d
Debts	£30
Hay and a furze rick	£2
Total	£59 4s 6d
	(£59.23)

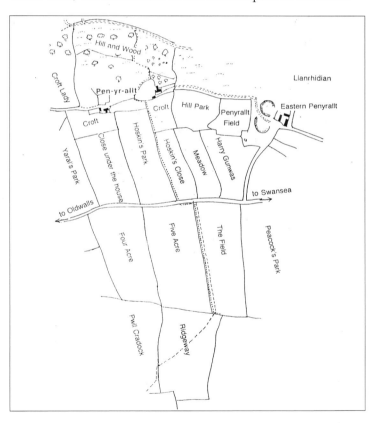

Penrallt Farm as it was up to the turn of this century. The division between east and west farms is marked by the dotted line running north-south across the map. The shape of the fields strongly suggests the enclosing of what were, originally, common field strips held by the villagers of Llanrhidian.

2. Pencaerfenni Farm

Pencaerfenni, 'the point of the wet field' its likeliest meaning, is placed very differently to Penrallt. On low and relatively infertile ground, it spread across 40 acres of the Welsh part of the parish. It was first mentioned in 1584 and was not an enclosure of presently existing common fields but rather a colonisation of new land, wet and intractable. The field names 'Waun Dunkin, 'Waun y Kipmon', 'Gags' and 'Llwyn Du' speak of poor, wet and scrubby land. Probably, it first covered most of the area now known as Crofty but was later split up into Pencaerfenni and Pencaerfenni Fach. The latter, we might guess, became known as the Crofty Farm. This would account for the diminution in the value of the property after the death of David Robert Hopkin in 1601. In his day, the farm concentrated on dairy cattle, sheep and arable farming with a large number of horses. A century later, under John David Hugh, it seemed to be changing to store cattle and pigs. Wills over the intervening period show this to be part of a trend. Attached to the farm were other lands in the Morlais area which were valuable for coal. It was, presumably, because of this that Robert Morris, a coal entrepreneur from the Welsh borders, purchased the farm in the 18th century and the farm passed through the hands of a number of wealthy people after that. Through this constant infusion of capital, Pencaerfenni came to have one of the most impressive 'suites' of farm buildings in the parish comprising in 1923 (at its sale) - the farm, a 5 stall stable, a calves house, cow house (20 cattle), cart and cattle sheds, 3 pig styes, a boiling house (for cockles), open air stalls and a stable.

Some of this survives today in the form of the present motel (now closed) and its outbuildings. The old pond, the lane to fields on Salthouse Point, the well in the adjacent field (used for watering ships coming up to Penclawdd in the 18th and 19th centuries), the old oakwood felled regularly for shipbuilding in Penclawdd, the little calves fields (Cae Lloi) opposite the farm and the track up to the big meadows (Maesydd) below Hermon Chapel are all now gone.

The barns of the old Pencaefenni farm survive having been converted into rooms for a motel in the 1970s

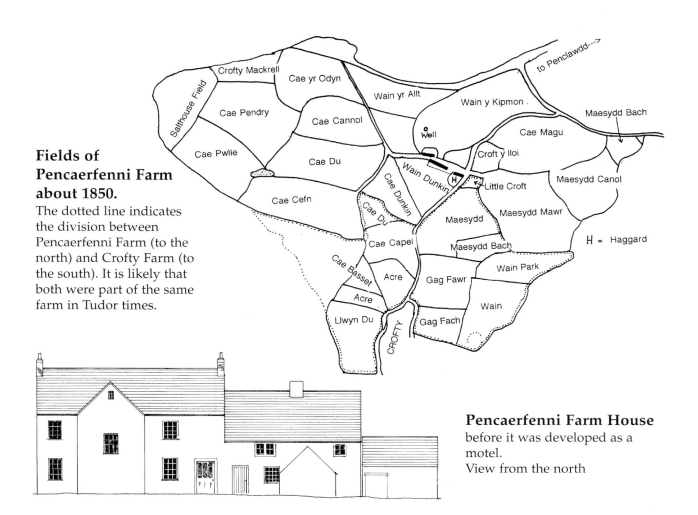

Fields of Pencaerfenni Farm about 1850.

The dotted line indicates the division between Pencaerfenni Farm (to the north) and Crofty Farm (to the south). It is likely that both were part of the same farm in Tudor times.

to Penclawdd-->
Crofty Mackrell
Cae yr Odyn
Salthouse Field
Wain yr Allt
Wain y Kipmon
Cae Pendry
Cae Cannol
Maesydd Bach
Well
Cae Magu
Cae Pwlle
Cae Du
Croft y lloi
Wain Dunkin
Cae Dunkin
H
Little Croft
Maesydd Canol
Cae Cefn
Cae Du
Maesydd
Maesydd Mawr
Cae Capel
Maesydd Bach
H = Haggard
Cae Basset
Acre
Wain Park
Gag Fawr
Acre
Wain
Llwyn Du
Gag Fach
CROFTY

Pencaerfenni Farm House

before it was developed as a motel.
View from the north

The Farm c1900

A - main farmhouse
B - cartshed
C - orchard
D - cowhouse
E - 'engine house'
F - calf house
G - 'Haggard Cottage' - site of the hayricks
H - barn
I - pig styes
J - lane leading to main meadows - survives today as a gap between houses
K - well used by estuary shipping to replenish water supplies
L - old tramway from colliery at Llanmorlais c1789

K
Wain y Kipmon
Wain yr allt
to Penclawdd
Cae Magu
H
I
POND
C
3
Croft y lloi
D
B
E
F
J
A
L
Wain Dunkin
G
Little Croft
Maesydd Mawr
to Crofty
Maesydd

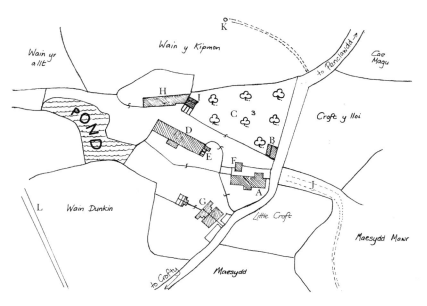

Llanrhidian Church - the parish's
most picturesque and ancient
religious building

The present church at
Llanyrnewydd (built 1850) stands
by the site of an older, possibly
medieval, building.

Llanrhidian Worships

There is no doubt of the early origins of church worship in Llanrhidian with medieval churches and chapels spread across the parish. Apart from Llanrhidian church (qv) itself there were chapels at Walterston and Llanyrnewyr (now Llanyrnewydd). Both these were effectively chapels-of-ease in far flung corners of the parish; this status was officially confirmed for Llanyrnewyr in 1587 when the inhabitants of the higher division were exempted from having to attend the church at Llanrhidian village. The appearance of the old chapel-of-ease at Llanyrnewyr can now, unfortunately, only be guessed but it was probably a rude building of a simple hall structure with, perhaps, a simple belfry on one gable end. It is a pattern often seen elsewhere in south Wales. This chapel was, however, poorly served and services tended to be held just once a month. In the Penclawdd area this produced both apathy and resentment so it is not surprising that the seeds of non-conformity were found in the higher part of the parish. It would be fair to say that the industrialisation of the area together with the established church's slow response created conditions in which non-conformity could flourish - a pattern copied across the country.

On the extreme fringes of the higher division lie the farms of Wimblewood. The farmers here were more likely to attend church at Ilston than either Llanyrnewyr or Llanrhidian - Wimblewood farmers were buried at Ilston. It is not surprising that they became linked with the Baptist church at Ilston and it may even be that John Miles, founder of the Welsh Baptist movement, had some property in the area in the period of Cromwell's rule. The later suppression of Puritanism did not succeed in stamping out non-conformity in the area. In 1673 the remote farmhouse of Tir Cethin, between Three Crosses and Penclawdd, was sanctioned as a place where services and preaching could be conducted. The equally obscure farm of Cwmmawr was likewise used in the period 1660-1689 and, around 1689, a small church was built there for non-conformist worship. In the lower division (c 1715) David Jones led a large community of non-conformists at Cilibion and Pilton. Congregations of 200 were recorded, drawn *'from all ranks of society'*.

In spite of these developments, the developing centre of Penclawdd was not a noted centre of religious fervour. In 1751 it was described by a local evangelist, Thomas William, as a *'dark and pagan place'* and it was more that 50 years after that when a chapel of any sort was built in its vicinity. The church at Cwmmawr, however, prospered and when its lease ran out (it is supposed) a new site was acquired in Three Crosses and the first Crwys chapel was built in 1788. This chapel, which belonged to the Congregational movement, was much smaller than the impressive building we see today. Like most of the chapels in the parish it was to be subject to modification and rebuilding.

The Baptist movement was still active in the area and in 1807, at the instigation of Joseph 'Gomer' Harris, a plot of land was acquired at the top of the Pencaerfenni Farm fields near Crofty for the erection of a small chapel - Hermon. This has stood since, unaltered, but sadly now in considerable ruin. But Penclawdd was still without a non-conformist place of worship to call its own. This was realised by the aristocratic evangelist Lady Barham who, in conjunction with the Calvinistic Methodist movement, established a non-conformist congregation from 1813 onwards. By 1816 a chapel called 'Bethel' had been erected in the heart of the old village.

Bethel Chapel as it is today after rebuilding in 1910.

The patronage of an English aristocrat sat uncomfortably with the congregation at 'Bethel' and tensions arose which were only assuaged by the calming influence of the Reverend Rees Jones, their minister. Not surprisingly, on his death there was a schism in the chapel which resulted in the more purist Calvinistic Methodist element leaving to form their own church. Thus was born Tabernacle Chapel on the sea front at Penclawdd (built 1836).

Meanwhile, the established church was awaking to the demands of its parishioners in the higher division. 'Chapel Sunday', when established church services were held in the ruinous little chapel-of-ease, came but once a month and local people were inclined to be critical of even that limited provision. The chapel, which had served the area for centuries, was demolished in 1850 to make way for a new building. Only the font seems to have survived. In Llanrhidian the old church was also decaying and substantial rebuilding of the old nave and south porch took place between 1856 and 1858.

Tabernacle, originally founded 1836, last rebuilt in 1911.

The Calvinistic Methodists continued to be the most thriving of local religious movements. Inhabitants of the western part of the higher division gained their own chapel of that denomination in 1844 when 'Penuel' was opened on the Rhallt. Near Oldwalls, 'Ebenezer' was erected in 1852 - the only non-conformist building in the lower division. There had clearly been a thriving community to support this venture since a Sunday School had been run by the Methodists in Oldwalls since 1825. Another Calvinistic Methodist community was developing in Crofty which opened its own chapel in 1884. This was associated with the rapid growth of the industrial population throughout the higher division in the latter half of the 19th century.

All denominations were now trying to keep apace with the demand for religion. The Baptists had a grand new building in the very heart of the old village of Penclawdd in the garden of their minister, John Williams. The new building, 'Trinity', was opened in 1867 and became eponymous with the old lane that ran past it up to Llotrog. 'Bethel' felt the need to establish a schoolroom-cum-chapel in the higher part of Penclawdd and opened 'Capel Isaac' in 1884 (demolished 1997). The survival of 'Bethel' after the schism of 1829 was largely due to the patronage of the chapel at Crwys which continued to flourish throughout this period. It, too, opened schoolrooms at Wern-olau (1861) and Cilonnen (Carmel - 1885).

Carmel, built 1885, a product of the flourishing non-conformist community at Crwys.

Crwys Chapel was itself becoming inadequate to the demands placed on the building and plans were laid to build a new chapel alongside it.

The famous John Humphrey of Morriston, architect of Morriston 'Tabernacle', designed the new building which is substantially that which we see today.

As the chapels continued to expand in numbers they took on extensive rebuilding and modification of their buildings. Bethel, Penuel and Tabernacle all rebuilt or remodelled their buildings. A final round of building about the turn of the century was the last ecclesiatical expansion to be seen in the area. The Baptists built 'Tirzah' (1906) in Llanmorlais whilst the established church built new chapels or 'mission halls' at Penclawdd(1910) and Wernffrwd (1898). The Penclawdd hall was on the site, and probably an extension, of an earlier structure which housed the local 'ranters' or Primitive Methodists.

The buildings alone have added sigificantly to the appearance of the villages of Llanrhidian but this is but a small part of the contribution they have played. They have served as centres of worship, as centres of sustenance in hard times, as centres of culture and eisteddfodau. They represent both the oldest and most consistent traditions within the area.

Zoar, in the heart of Crofty.

Ebenezer, the only non-conformist building of the lower division.

Trinity, the Baptist chapel built in the back garden of its pastor John Williams in 1867.

The mission chapel built by the Church of Wales by the marsh at Wernffrwd in 1898.

Tirzah, a Baptist foundation, was the last ecclesiatical building erected in the parish

Llanrhidian at School

A humble yeoman such as Philip Hopkin of Crofty (died 1625) ensured the education of his grandchildren during their minority by providing finance for tutors. Anthony Gwynne (died 1663), the miller of Llanrhidian, desired that his children be *'cept att skoole for to reead'* and set aside some of the rent of the mill *'to pay for there lerninge'*. Such schooling was probably obtained in Swansea. Most people in the parish, however, were in no position to purchase learning and remained illiterate. It was the purpose of the circulating schools of Griffith Jones to alleviate this situation. The first of these schools came to the area in 1741/2 when a circulating school operated at Llanyrnewydd and 120 pupils attended. During the next two years the schools visited Llanrhidian (74 pupils) and Windmill Farm (66 pupils) near Weobley. In 1745 and 1746 a circulating school was held at *'Welch Moor in Llanrhidian'* (66 and 49 pupils) and in 1747 another at *'Dunfant in Llanrhidian'* (18 pupils). Madame Bevan of Laugharne took up the patronage of the circulating schools after Griffith Jones's death and a further school was held in Penclawdd in 1767 (37 pupils). Thomas Clement is recorded in the following decade as being a schoolmaster of the parish but apart from this there is no indication that any institutionalised education took place in the parish in the closing decades of the 18th century.

Village tradition in Penclawdd has it otherwise. Sue Gronow's 'dame school' was founded, according to this tradition, as a result of her arriving in the village in the 1790's with her new husband John Gronow. They purchased a little thatched cottage at the foot of the hill between the old village and Llotrog and shortly began a school. The Commissioners' report of 1847 does not reflect this as an accurate account, however, and suggests that Mrs Gronow was born at the turn of the century and did not open her academy until 1845. It further states that the school was a 'church' school although Mrs Gronow was dependent, as most teachers in the area, on her 'school pence' for income. It may be that Sue Gronow's mother arrived in the circumstances of the tradition and showed an early interest in education which was fostered by her daughter. There were dame schools in other parts of the parish - at Wernffrwd and at Crwys (opposite the Post Office). The earliest authenticated regular day school was, in fact, that of the Calvinistic Methodists which began two years after their Sunday School at Oldwalls in 1825. In 1845 it was run by Maria Allen of Stoneyford and received some commendation from the inspector (as did Sue Gronow in her school) as a *'useful school for reading and writing'*. Miss Allen's pupils, of whom there were 16, were mostly over 10 years of age and for the most part literate. In Three Crosses, however, the Reverend John Evans, minister of Crwys, ran the 'Crwys Academy' between 1819 and 1856 - among the subjects taught were navigation, astronomy and divinity. Sue Gronow's 28 pupils were almost entirely between 5 and 10; only 6 of them seemed to be reading. Clearly, these institutions, worthy as they may have been, were not capable of meeting the educational

Penclawdd School as it was built in 1843 (based on a plan in Swansea Archive Office).

Llanforlais School

Crwys School

Penclawdd Junior School, built 1876, in the process of being demolished in 1991 after the school had reopened in the old secondary school.

needs of the parish. This need was met, primarily, when the church established a school in Penclawdd (in 1843) and another in Llanrhidian (in 1845). The Penclawdd school, at Banc Bach in the old village, was opened under the patronage of Starling Benson and a Mr C Morgan (who may have been Charles Morgan of *Cae Forgan*, near Cillibion). It was attended, in 1847, by 74 pupils. The bulk of the pupils was aged between 5 and 10 but there were 20 under 5 and 16 over 10. Less than half of all pupils could read. The Llanrhidian School was no more successful with its 22 pupils who were mostly between 5 and 10 years of age. Mr Grant, the master, appeared to be 'diligent' and the children 'orderly but ignorant', their attendenace 'short but irregular'. This first school in Llanrhidian was built on the site now occupied in the heart of the village by the church hall. A brief account of the state of schools in 1847 should include Mr Morris's rather unsuccessful academy in Penuel Chapel where only 2 out of the 8 rather disorderly pupils could read. The inspector's comments for the parish, on the whole, reflect classrooms that were dusty and under-equipped, children who were dirty and poorly educated by teachers struggling with little training and poor resources.

It might be thought that the paucity of educational provision in the area would be remedied by the strength of Sunday schools. Numerically, these were far stronger than the day schools and predominantly non-conformist. Lady Barham had started a Sunday school as early as 1814. Crwys Chapel had followed in 1818 and more followed at Oldwalls (1825), Tycoch Farm (1829), Penuel (1831), Hermon (1836), Penclawdd (1838), Berthlwyd (1841), Wimblewood (1842) and Llanrhidian Church (1846). There were 555 persons on roll in these schools of whom 480 were attending at the 1847 inspection. But the quality of the education being offered was questionable; it seems that the statistics were more impressive than the reality.

The improvement of schooling in the parish depended very much on the improvement of the day schools and these, in turn, relied heavily on the support from central government in legislation and finance. So it was only gradually that the educational service expanded with the Penclawdd School coming under the National Schools movement (apparently in 1863) and then moving into new, purpose-built, premises at Dalton's Point in 1876. Although the new school was designed to hold 400 students it was apparent at the outset that teaching the infants alongside the older children presented major practical difficulties in the building. This was resolved in 1910 when a splendid new infants school was opened in Banc Bach. Pupils graduating beyond these village schools had to go to Gowerton and this has remained the case to the present day except for a period when a secondary-modern school was opened in 'The Park' behind the old Ship and Castle public house. When Gowerton School became comprehensive the Penclawdd secondary school became a part of its split-site and accommodated the lower years. In time it was perceived as being undesirable to run a school operating on three sites spread over as many miles. The school was closed and reopened in 1989, imaginatively, as a splendid site for a combined junior and infants school in the village. The 1876 junior school was subsequently demolished and the infants school converted into a community centre. The new school, consequently, has generous premises which make it a model for enlightened primary school provision.

The primary school at Llanmorlais was opened in 1893 in response to the rapidly growing population of the area. The school has thrived since and survived rationalisation plans that would have led to its closure in the 1980's. Dunvant gained a primary school in 1877 whilst Crwys Primary School opened in 1875 opposite the site of Crwys Chapel. The village has expanded significantly during the 20th century and the school buildings show their limitations, as the millenium approaches, in their size and facilities. The problems created are an example of how Penclawdd has come to dominate the parish in size and in its ability, as a result, to draw in the lion's share of investment in services. Whilst Three Crosses has grown out of all recognition from its original scattering of farms and labourers cottages, its services have not kept pace.

THE SCHOOL, LLANRHIDIAN.

The present school at Llanrhidian is on a new site at the top of the village. The old school was built by the church on the site of the hall immediately above the church where Mr Grant taught 'orderly but ignorant' pupils in 1847.

Cockles

No aspect of the story of Llanrhidian is more talked about or so little documented as that of the business of cockles. Nor is any aspect of the history of the area taken to be so typical. In the early days no rents or leases were needed to work on the sands, no buildings required for the processing of the cockles, no special arrangements needed for their transport to market, no special shops for their sale. In fact, the whole industry was carried on in what would be regarded today as an informal way and as a consequence there are no written documents or accounts relating to the cockle industry until, in the middle of the last century, it came to be regarded as picturesque and worthy of note to travellers. To ask when the industry began is the same as to ask when people first settled the area because gathering cockles (and other food) from the estuary has always been a part of life here. The important period in the industry was when the cockles began to be gathered as a supplement to income as well as a supplement to diet. We can only make informed guesses as to when this began to happen. It was not until the early 18th century that the local industrial economy 'took-off'. This would have brought an influx of workers who could not always rely on employment in mines and would need, as a consequence, to have an alternative source of income. Local farmers and fishermen, too, may have realised that there was now available a new workforce capable of extracting cockles in sufficient numbers to supply the market in Swansea. In 1810 it was observed that *'most of the females are employed in gathering cockles'* and it is likely that this had been the case for some decades previously.

The traditional cockle seller would have been seen about the streets of Swansea and many other towns in south Wales.

There are two notable features of the cockle business - the fact that it was predominantly carried on by women and the fact that it was an unremittingly hard and wearisome business. It is difficult to say what was the effect of so many women being able to earn a separate income from their husbands - it would certainly have been unusual and may have bred an independence of spirit unique to the area. It may also have made it difficult for the better-off inhabitants to secure servants because many women would have preferred to work 'on the sands' - this may, in turn, have had the effect of slightly improving wages for people in service. Whatever the truth of these speculations, the hardiness of those women who scraped and seived day-after-day on the cold and windswept estuary is beyond doubt. They sallied forth from the front at Penclawdd, Salthouse Point at Crofty and from Wernffrwd to harvest the shells. At times they would go beyond the sands of the south side of the estuary as far as Cefn Sidan or even Ferryside or Laugharne. This would often involve weeks away from home for many of the pickers since to travel thus far each day made too great a demand on them and their animals. The animals in the last century were mainly donkeys and they were kept in such prodigious numbers on waste land around the villages that the hillsides were known to reverberate with their braying all through the night. Illustrations of the last century also indicate that ponies were used and, until recent years, ponies have been the mainstay of the gatherers this century.

The first picture is from the 'Illustrated Weekly News' 1867. Nearly a hundred years later, the next picture shows that processing practices had changed little.

The use of donkeys has been superseded first by ponies with carts and now by four-wheel-drive vehicles and, occasionally, by vessels equipped to draw the cockles up by mechanical fishing techniques.

The ladies who worked on the sand were often photographed in scenes to display their customary dress and accoutrements. In these prictures the traditional baskets, woven in Penclawdd and unique to the village, can also be seen.

Cockles are now cooked in a highly specialised process that meets stringent health requirements but in earlier times they were simply boiled up on crude stoves erected from a few stones and some metal bars. In the 1870's some twenty or more of these were seen along the seafront near the Royal Oak. Around the village there were other locations where boiling could take place. On the busiest days, Fridays, towards the end of the 19th century, Penclawdd must have been an extraordinary sight and smell. Steam would rise from numbers of stoves as well as from the factories and mines. Mixed with the reek of the metal works would have been the distinctive fresh fish smell of the cockles. Overall there would have been a buzz of human activity the like of which has not been seen in the village since.

Cockles were sent primarily to Swansea to be marketed by hawking them through the streets. It was the Saturday sales of cockles that provided the extra income that could improve the quality of life for Penclawdd families. Returning from town on a Saturday evening on the 'relish train' the women were awaited by their families with real hope and expectancy. On a good day the local populace must have thought themselves blessed to be living in a place that could provide for them in so many ways. Before the railway, the women walked to Swansea with their loads. They stopped at Olchfa ('the washing place') or St David's Ditch running below Sketty (now the entrance to Singleton Park) to wash their feet and don their shoes. Bringing cockles to market on foot surely restricted the quantity they could bring so the arrival of rail transport made a great difference to them. It also meant that fresh cockles could be sent further afield and this led to another aspect of the business. Many of the girls and women were sent away to lodge in the valleys or the larger towns to the east of Swansea where they could receive deliveries by rail and market them in the town where they resided. At its height, the cockle industry was extensive and complex and contributed very significantly to the local economy. It has since proved more enduring than any other industry.

The Final Chapter

During the course of the nineteenth century the two halves of the parish, higher and lower, became so different that they could no longer be regarded as part of the same entity. This difference has been perpetuated and conserved through local authority planning and policy. The lower division, now a separate community, is completely rural and without any significant housing development. As a result it is still one of the most beautiful parts of the Gower peninsula - preserving much of its original character and atmosphere. The higher division, on the other hand, has continued to expand in terms of housing, particularly in the Crofty area, developing as a dormitory district for Swansea. However, the industrialism of the nineteenth century which appeared to be turning Penclawdd and its environs into another Llanelli or Gorseinon, has somewhat receded. Around 1880 Penclawdd was at its height. The railway ran through the village with the frequent sound of coal trucks clinking and trundling, engines shunting and taking the coal off to wider markets. The tinplate works and the old copper works were in full production, the sound of the hammers and mills echoing across the houses, the smell of the furnaces pervading the atmosphere. Up on the hill and east and west of the village, coal mines were busy and winding gear worked all day long. Along the foreshore the women were boiling their cockles and up on the hill side, especially at night, the donkeys brayed incessantly. The village shops and inns were busy victualling the population of nearly 4000, the sound of horse, cart and human feet constantly grinding the gritty roads.

During the first decade of the twentieth century the metal works fell idle for the last time and have since been almost entirely demolished. Coal mining, also, has completely ceased. Throughout Wales the coal industry reached a peak before the First World War which has never been attained since. In Llanrhidian parish the mines began to close as that peak was passed. The Llanmorlais colliery, for example, closed finally in 1917. The Wernbwll never recovered after the 1929 explosion and closed in 1930. The Wern colliery, extended by workings close to Gelli-orllwyn Farm, closed in 1935. A slight increase in activity during the Second World War led to some workings producing low grade coal as at Gelligroes but the last workings, at Llanyrnewydd, were principally engaged in excavating fireclay and closed in 1950. Not surprisingly, the railway did not survive the decline of industry. Passenger services had ceased long before the last war and the rails were finally lifted in the winter of 1959 to 1960.

The symptoms of decline can be seen in many facets of the life of the community and yet it has maintained its population and its identity. The chapels and churches have remained active and are still a vital part of the social fabric of the area. The major chapels - Crwys, Bethel and Tabernacle - have been able to maintain their material fabric to an admirable degree although no new structures have been attempted since 1911. The cockle trade thrives on the sands although, with increasing mechanisation, employing rather fewer people than in the past. This is a forward-looking industry that has sought to meet new standards in

One wall of the old copper works still survives in a Penclawdd garden.

A new cockle processing factory at Crofty.

quality and hygiene and to survive strenuous European Community regulations. During the 1990's there has been substantial investment in new processing plant, especially at Llanmorlais and Crofty. At the same time the conservation of the beds has been rigorously controlled and rights to gather cockles are jealously guarded. Changes in financing fishery controls presently threaten this state of affairs.

The sale of Pencaerfenni Farm before the war was to have far reaching effects. A Royal Ordnance factory was built on the promontory west of the farm and this was active during the war. After the war the factory became disused but the site was acquired for industrial and building purposes. The Crofty Industrial Estate began in the 1950's as a rather ramshackle development allowing low grade industrial premises. At the same time the more southerly farmlands on the promontory were sold for housing and the Pencaerfenni Estate was begun in 1968. This now, in effect, extends the whole length of the promontory almost as far as the sewage works on Salthouse Point. The parallel development of housing and industry inevitably led to some friction during the 1970's. The need to improve tidiness and planning in the industrial estate became pressing as residents became unhappy at some of the developments. These included light engineering, warehouse facilities, plastic manufacture, car spraying and repair and scrap retrieval. The industrial estate at Crofty is now the major employer within the parish so that expectations of limiting its impact on the environment have to be reconciled with the economic contribution it makes to the community.

Pencaerfenni is but one of a number of housing estates in the area. In 1976 an estate was begun on the adjacent Cae Capel called 'Rhyd y Fenni'. In the previous few years there had been smaller developments in Llanmorlais and in Penclawdd, notably on the site of the old Coed Farm at Graig y Coed. At the other end of Penclawdd, expansion has gone on over 20 years on the fields of the long lost Abercedi Farm. Waun y Felin and Glan y Lli are the result of two separate developments more or less completed by the mid 1990's. No community has been more transformed, however, by housing developments than Three Crosses. At the turn of the century it consisted of little more than scattered workmen's cottages and small farms. It is now a major area of new housing. The main areas of development are on the Gowerton Road and in the triangle of land between the roads that create the eponymous three crosses. Development on the Gowerton road is more or less of a 'ribbon' nature and quite piecemeal in character whereas the area in the 'triangle', along Pant y Dwr and Llwyn Derw for example, has been developed in a more planned manner.

Local council building has been less conspicuous in the parish but has played a significant role in providing decent housing for everyone. Developments are mainly small and quite unobtrusive as at Malt Hall in Llanrhidian, Abercedi in Penclawdd and Bryn y Mor in Three Crosses. Housing was built by the Gower Rural District Council immediately after the Second World War in response to the massive increase in demand for homes. This was particularly acute in Penclawdd where the relatively large Caban Isaac development took place from 1946 onwards. Houses here were built at a cost of £60 to £200 per home. By 1948 the main

Local authority housing at Malt Hall, Llanrhidian.

acquisition of sites had taken place in Dunvant, Three Crosses, Penclawdd, Crofty and Llanrhidian. The development in the heart of Crofty, Westbourne Terrace, consists of just 12 semi-detached homes - a far more sensitive addition to the village than the private developments of the 1970's. The Llanyrnewydd estate around the old Caban Isaac is much larger but, sited on the crest of Graig Penclawdd, remains unobtrusive and a natural extension of the developing village.

Local authority housing at Crofty - Westbourne Terrace.

An important part of the social structure of the communities of the area in the first half of the twentieth century were the Welfare Committees. Originating as 'Miner's Welfare Committees', they were able to raise funds to create facilities for the community as a whole and have left their mark in both Penclawdd, Three Crosses and Llanmorlais. Indeed, at the time of writing the Welfare Committee is still active in Llanmorlais where the village hall was built and is run entirely from funds raised and secured by itself. In Crofty and Llanmorlais it remains crucial to the social life of the community. Earlier in the century, the committee secured land for the building of a village hall and for sporting activities for which it is still used. The village carnival, as well as being a celebration of the community, is a vital part of fund raising for the committee. In Penclawdd, the Welfare Committee was absorbed into the community council in 1973 during local government reorganisation. As a result, the council has acquired the assets of the committee in the form of the 'recreation ground' (used by the Penclawdd Rugby Football Club) and the Memorial Hall and Gardens. Similarly, the Miner's Welfare Pavilion at Three Crosses is now rebuilt and maintained by the Community Council. It has not proved an easy task for a community council to administer these assets in the spirit of the old Welfare Committee.

As a result of the efforts of the committees in the earlier part of the century, the leisure activities of the post-war communities are now relatively well served. The Penclawdd 'Welfare' lands now provide facilities for rugby, bowls and tennis; in Llanmorlais they provide for soccer, tennis and carnival days. The communities take great pride in the successes of their sporting teams, as they did in the past. The quoits teams of Penclawdd and Crofty are still remembered with particular pride by older members of the community. The village halls also provide for important community activites. In Llanmorlais the village hall was built on the basis of local subscription but in Three Crosses the small pavilion was an early product of the work of the Llanrhidian Higher Community Council. In Penclawdd the old infants school was converted to use as a community hall in 1990 as a result of funding from Swansea District Council. All these centres provide for Women's Institutes, Gardening Clubs, Health Clubs, Badminton sessions, educational courses, a Heritage Association, Senior Citizens' Groups and a number of other activities. The particular success of the Penclawdd Brass Band in the latter half of the century has been due to the dedication and expertise of its members, led by Mr Tony Small. The efforts of the band have secured them a small 'band hut' adjacent to the village primary school. On a balmy evening the sounds of the band practising in its 'hut', the rugby team practising on the nearby fields, the local choir singing in the

The community hall at Llanmorlais was built entirely through the efforts and resources of local people

119

Where higher and lower divisions meet, the marsh remains the landscape element common to both parts of the parish.

school and club members arriving at the nearby community centre give an impression of the lively and active community that is Penclawdd as the millenium approaches.

Llanrhidian is now a divided parish with a common heritage. The old village in the lower division is by no means declining - it is an active community that preserves successfully the character of this old part of the parish. Between the two halves of Llanrhidian can be seen much that is typical of Wales - past and present, rural and urban, higher and lower.

The Community Councils of the Lower (left) and Higher (right) Divisions continue to be important in the administration and provision of local facilities.

Appendix 1

POPULATION FIGURES

The first figures available for measuring population in Llanrhidian date from Tudor times when subsidy and tax assessments were based on the number of households. Unfortunately these figures, like many after, excluded a large part of the populace who were too poor to pay tax. We are thus left with estimations based on the number of persons per tax paying household (on average between 4.3 and 5.6) added to a reasoned guess as to the number of non-taxpayers. From 1801 onwards figures became much more reliable and the 10 yearly census became established. The spectacular rise of population in the higher division during the 19th century is very apparent. The second graph shows how the population responded to different stimuli or inhibiting influences during the period 1801 to 1911.

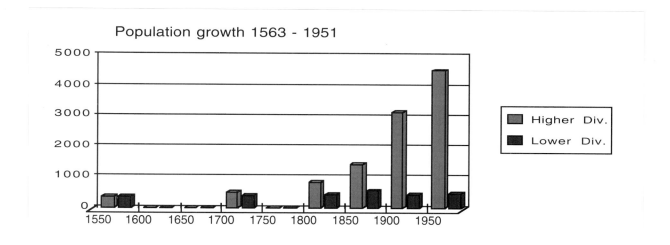

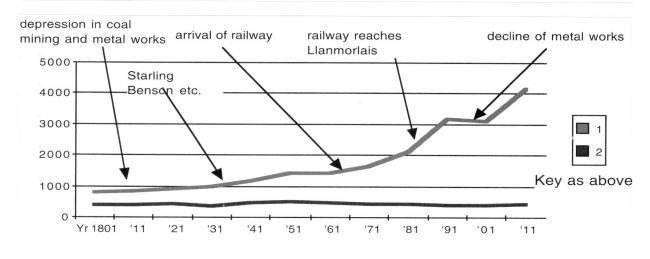

Population changes from 1801 to 1911

Appendix 2 - Llethryd

The Way to Wernhalog

The following text, from Clark's *Cartae et Munimentae de Glamorgan* (no.4314 on page 1699) makes incidental mention of many places in Llanrhidian, including a reference to what appears to be 'Black Lane' running from Llethrid to Wernhalog, in addition to a dramatic resolution of a legal wrangle that might appeal to today's solicitors.

An Indenture made 16th November 1472 (12 Edward VI)

Showing that whereas John Mauncell of Leisonston of the one part and Hugh Owen of the same of the other part were bound in £20 to abide the award of Oweyn ap Jenkyn ap Henry, Nicholle Philippe, Hopkyn Skynner, and Richard Scurlac, in their dispute concerning title to 5 acres of land and 10 acres wood in Leisonston felde, the said arbitrators not agreeing, Hopkin ap David was chosen umpire, who adjudged that the seyde John shall swer to the seyd Hugh in the chirche of Langenyth upon Saint Kenyth is hedde, and ye seyde Hugh to bring fourth the relike by tyme nine at bell in ye mornynge and three at afternoon a Sunday the 21st day of March next, the seyd John and eleven fre holders with hym by West pulle as Llythred ledyth to Sir John Walter is place in Wernhaloc, and swere that his title of the seyde Hugh Owayn by his deedes of purchase .....

Llethryd Acid Works

The Llethryd Acid Works were Active towards the end of the 19th century and some remains are visible in the woods immediately north of today's hamlet (grid ref. 531915). In 1883 they were described as follows:-

'... in the foreground of woded hills near Llethryd are works of Messrs. Vivian and Sons for the distillation of acid from ligneous matter, to which the pungent smell bears ample testimony'.

(Source - 'A Complete and Reliable Guide to Swansea and the Mumbles. Gower', James C Woods 1883)

The remains of the Lethrid Acid Works

Appendix 3 Employment in 1851————————

The graphs below show the numbers of men and women employed in Llanrhidian in various trades and occupations. Seen side-by-side, there are striking differences between the two halves of Llanrhidian and the industrial nature of the higher division shows up well. It is noticeable, however, that the agricultural aspect of the economy remained strong in the higher division (though by percentage it was not as strong as in the lower division). Social historians will note the extreme importance of 'service' as an employment for both men and women (principally women). Figures for servants include 'farm servants'.

It should be noted that some occupations are not shown on the graph because only one person is recorded altogether in that occupation. For interest, these occupations were as follows :-

> **Lower division** - hat-maker, shipwright, cooper, horsebreaker.
> **Higher division** - quarryman, patternmaker, fireman, timekeeper, wheelwright, boatman, merchant, postwoman, carrier, cabinet maker, coastwaiter (customs).

Philip Evans of Brynhir professed himself as a landed proprietor (he also owned Pencaerfenni Farm). Only one manager, that of the copper works, was living in the parish at the time of the census on which these statistics are based.

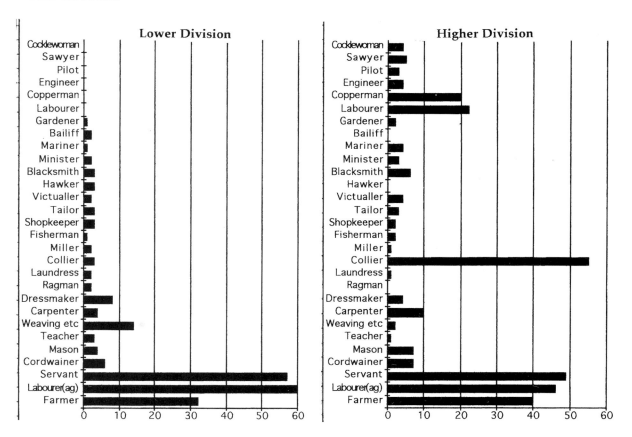

Bibliography

Primary Sources
Court Book for Subboscus and other papers held in the *Badminton Collection* held at the National Library of Wales
Mayberry Papers held at the National Library of Wales
Penrice and Margam Estate Papers held at the National Library of Wales and in the West Glamorgan Archives
The collection of wills relating to residents of the parish held at the National Library of Wales
Census returns for the parish from 1841 onwards held at Swansea Reference Library
The Cambrian held in index and microfilm at Swansea Central Library
Tithe maps and schedules held at Swansea Central Library
Briton Ferry Estate Papers held in the West Glamorgan Archives
Letter Books of the customs authgorieties of Swansea and Llanelli held at the Public Record Office in Kew

Secondary Sources
Bayliffe, Dorothy and Harding, Joan : *Starling Benson of Swansea* (1996)
Cooper, R N : *A Dark and Pagan Place* (1986)
Lucas, Robert: *A Gower Family* (1986)
Jones, Wyn: *The History of Capel y Crwys, Gower* (1988)
Orrin, Geoffrey: *The Gower Churches* (1979)
(For a wide range of other sources see the bibliography of *A Dark and Pagan Place* above from which the present work has drawn extensively and thus used indirectly)

Journals
Gower - the journal of the Gower society, has been a constant and invaluable aid to local history in Gower. In particular I would like to give recognition to the following recent contributions - the Gower Magazine number given in brackets after each title.
Morgan, Prys: *Music Making in Gower Houses in the Early Nineteenth Century* (43)
Taylor, Bryan S: *The Watermills of Gower* (42)
Rees, David: *Walterston: An Old Gower Settlement* (35)
Rees, David: *The Gower Estates of Sir Rhys ap Thomas* (43)
Schlesinger, Alex et al: *Excavations at Llanelen, Llanrhidian* (46)
Toft, L A *"To the Vill of Penmaen"* (40)
Toft, L A: *Walterston* (47)
Toft, L A: *The Celtic Church Monuments of Gower* (35)

Also -
Alex Schlesinger, Colin Walls, with Jonathan Kissock, Chris Lovegrove, Kate Pollard and Nick Wright: *An early church and medieval farmstead site: excavations at Llanelen* Gower Archaeological Journal 153 (1996)

Index of Names

Index of Names

General Index

General Index